advance praise for *Business Class*

"A much-needed primer for professionals in today's business environment because, whether you realize it or not, good manners and proper protocol can make or break a promising business relationship."   —Tony Alessandra, Ph.D., coauthor of *The Platinum Rule*

"How you treat others and how you conduct yourself are not casual imperatives. They are important, and if you agree, then this engagingly written book ought to entice you to its pages."
    —Jack Valenti, former president of the
    Motion Picture Association of America

"Readable, spirited, and chock-full of excellent information. Anyone in business, at the bottom or at the top, could benefit from this book."   —Letitia Baldrige, author of *New Manners for New Times: A Complete Guide to Etiquette* and former White House Social Secretary in the Kennedy Administration

"Fills a gaping void in contemporary business leadership grooming and constitutes an overdue and easy primer for success-oriented commercial leaders."
    —General Alexander M. Haig, Jr., former White House
    Chief of Staff, former NATO Commander, and former
    U.S. Secretary of State

"People make decisions about you based on your manners and comportment; this book shows you how to make and maintain a positive impression every time."

—Brian Tracy, author of *TurboStrategy: 21 Powerful Ways to Transform Your Business and Boost Your Profits Quickly*

"A practical, straightforward, commonsense guide to essential business conduct."

—Joanne Gordon, author of *Be Happy at Work: 100 Women Who Love Their Jobs, and Why*

"A treasure of how-to's about being a thoughtful, sensitive, and effective human being."

—Judy B. Rosener, Ph.D., author of *America's Competitive Secret: Women Managers* and professor at the graduate school of management, University of California, Irvine

"An invaluable guide filled with helpful etiquette solutions for your personal and professional life."

—Charles P. Garcia, CEO of Sterling Financial Investment Group

"A must-read book for all business operations, small or large, that depend on a clientele and employee attitude to make the difference between profit and loss."

—Lee Ellis, former vice president of CBS and Gannett Publications *(USA Weekend)*

"Whitmore covers everything from e-mail to formal dinner parties with a warm, friendly style that makes reading the book enjoyable and remembering her advice easy."

—Carolyn B. Elman, CEO of American Business Women's Association

BUSINESS *Class*

etiquette

essentials

for success

at work

JACQUELINE WHITMORE

ST. MARTIN'S PRESS  New York

www.stmartins.com

Design by Ruth Lee-Mui

Library of Congress Cataloging-in-Publication Data

Whitmore, Jacqueline.
    Business class : etiquette essentials for success at work / Jacqueline
Whitmore.
        p. cm.
Includes bibliographical references (p. 159) and index (p. 169).
    ISBN 0-312-33809-0
    EAN 978-0-312-33809-1
    1. Business etiquette.   I. Title

HF5389.W46 2005
395.5'2—dc22

                                                      2005042026

First Edition: July 2005

10   9   8   7   6   5   4   3   2   1

This book is dedicated to my mother,

ELSIE WHITMORE,

who is my best etiquette teacher.
She doesn't teach me, she shows me.

contents

foreword

Jacqueline Whitmore gets it. And "it" is critical to all of us.

I learned this by divine accident. This true story begins one afternoon in the spring of 2003. I had just returned to Minneapolis after giving a speech in Miami, and as I walked into my health club I was plagued by the thought that my speech was missing something. I knew I'd imparted some useful lessons on marketing and client relationships, but I was equally certain that the audience—and I—needed more.

What we needed was a better understanding of the simple acts that bind us together, of the acts that make civilization just that: civilized. How should we act to make others feel valued—and to ensure that they do not feel the opposite?

That thought brought back to me a memory. It was of being a young man watching the last night of a remarkable PBS series called *Civilization*, hosted by Kenneth Clark. Only a couple minutes remained in the program, so everyone watching knew that Clark was about to sum up. We were about to hear something profound about where we had been and where we might be heading.

I still remember his exact preface: "I also hold one or two beliefs that are more difficult to put simply."

And then it came.

"For example," he said, "I believe in courtesy, the ritual by which we avoid hurting other people's feelings by satisfying our own egos."

Those words were tumbling around in my head when I arrived at a bench in the club and sat down to survey the rack of hand weights in front of me. I looked above the rack into the mirror and noticed a woman approaching, with an obvious sense of purpose, from across the room. I realized that her purpose was to come say something to me. I was right.

"I just wanted to introduce myself," she said, "because my husband and I see you here often and wanted to address you by name."

I sensed that somehow there was a connection between Clark's words in my head and this woman. I was right again. I quickly learned that she taught etiquette in several Minneapolis public schools. I told her about my belief that I needed to incorporate etiquette into my teaching of adults. When she replied she said something else I've never forgotten: the word "mindfulness." "The course is called 'Manners and Mindfulness,'" she said, "because you cannot be mannerly without being mindful of others."

Of course. That was the first improvement I needed to make, and stress to my audiences: mindfulness.

This synchronicity of events did not end there. Just two mornings later, my phone rang. It was a Jacqueline Whitmore calling from Palm Beach, Florida. She had an intriguing and glamorous-sounding business title: international protocol consultant. I instantly pictured her sipping shaken martinis on a porch overlooking the harbor in Monte Carlo with a tuxedo-clad James Bond.

She was calling me because she thought my ideas on relating to others might be interesting to her clients. But all I could think about was this startling coincidence. Within hours, it seemed, my troubled message had passed through the air telepathically, landing first in Minneapolis and then bouncing east to a light in southeastern Florida. Here were some answers, the first steps to helping myself and others.

I hope everyone can reap the rewards that came to me from that divine conspiracy of events, and they can. They can read this book.

Like Jacqueline, I believe passionately in this subject. Perhaps that is a product of growing up near what business travelers once named as the most courteous city in North America: Portland, Oregon. But unlike Jacqueline, I fear I am far better at clinging to this belief than in acting upon it. So I was delighted to receive the manuscript that soon became this book, and even more pleased when I had finished it.

The lessons of marketing, sales, and business itself are incomplete without the lessons of this wonderful book. This idea of manners and courtesy is not something quaint, a notion that to some people may conjure up images of high teas, curtsies, and powdered wigs. This is something simpler and universal: a series of lessons in how to be a human being. In these times particularly, when people often seem so divided and at odds, it's hard to imagine lessons as timely and important, not to mention as well conveyed. This book gives us the chance, among other things, to make life more like the one promised by those bumper stickers: a series of random acts of kindness.

So thank you, Jacqueline, from one of what I hope are twenty million grateful readers.

Harry Beckwith

BUSINESS
Class

INTRODUCTION

> Prepare yourself for the world, as the athletes used to
> do for their exercise; oil your mind and your manners,
> to give them the necessary suppleness and flexibility;
> strength alone will not do.
>
> —LORD CHESTERFIELD,
> *British statesman, diplomat,*
> *and author*

R aw talent, education or experience, and compe-
tency are no longer enough to get a job, keep a job,
and advance in a job. Nor is it enough to have the
right product or service at the right time to court a client and land
the contract. Succeeding in today's global economy is oftentimes
measured by your ability to wield a fork like a European, mix and
mingle like a head of state, and build and sustain solid relationships like a seasoned CEO. More important, success comes when
you are able to put others at ease. It is a reflection of the ability to
get along well with all kinds of people, from the janitor who
works for your company to the mayor of your city.

Along with communicating, negotiating, and motivating,
business etiquette is an essential "soft skill" that separates the
leaders from the left behind. If you aren't in tune with how your

behavior affects others, you may be damaging valuable business relationships outside your company as well as within. Some people say that courtesy is just common sense, but what was once considered common sense is not so common anymore.

Good manners and subtle social graces are not inborn, they are learned. Etiquette and manners must be practiced just as you would practice tennis, golf, painting, or playing the piano. When you repeat a behavior often enough, it becomes automatic, feels natural, and helps you feel more confident in your abilities. When you exercise your business etiquette skills on a daily basis, you are better able to concentrate on the business at hand without anxiety about doing or saying something inappropriate or embarrassing.

A little polish and professionalism never hurt anyone in business. People of all levels, from college students to the brightest, highest-ranking executives, are signing up in droves for etiquette courses around the United States in order to learn the manners they might not have learned at home or at school. Many newly minted MBAs, middle managers, and CEOs alike are finding out that business etiquette courses help enhance their self-confidence and ability to interact with clients, customers, and coworkers with grace and aplomb.

One of my clients is a sales manager for an upscale resort and spa in Scottsdale, Arizona. He decided to invest in a business etiquette seminar so he could brush up on meeting and greeting people and finessing the business meal. "I have the manners my mother gave me, but they're not sufficient for today's ever-changing business world," he told me when he registered. He said he is moving up the corporate ladder so quickly, he regularly gets asked to represent his company at events where luminaries, dignitaries, and other high-profile guests are in attendance. "I want to know how to make a great impression in the event I'm invited to a state dinner at the White House or a casual barbecue with my colleagues," he said.

A few months after he took my seminar, he called to thank me and tell me that the lessons he learned gave him more confidence and made him more polished and well-rounded. "Before the seminar, I was looking for a way to distinguish myself from the competition," he told me. "Now etiquette is my secret weapon."

WHAT THIS BOOK WILL DO FOR YOU

To many, the word "etiquette" conjures up images of someone who is stuffy, old-fashioned, or pretentious. But etiquette is not about putting on airs, being artificial, or being better than anyone else. In the pages that follow, you'll discover that business etiquette isn't only for the upper crust or social climbers: it's a powerful, practical, and profitable skill you can use when it counts the most.

To win in today's competitive world of business, you have to know how to play the game. Of course, to excel in any game, you must know the rules. Etiquette is a set of rules and guidelines that make your personal and professional relationships more harmonious, productive, manageable, and meaningful. I've learned that the rules of etiquette, like most other rules for life or work, are not carved in stone. As I interviewed a great many bright, talented, and successful men and women for this book, I found that their anecdotes and words of wisdom were based largely on good judgment and good manners. These top executives' stories confirm that good manners translate into good business. Their classic concepts, practices, and suggestions may even inspire and help you outline your own blueprint for success.

At times their advice may surprise you and even contradict what you have read or have been taught in other etiquette books. But everyone I interviewed agreed that everything in life is situational and subject to choice, good taste, and appropriateness. How your colleague handles a particular situation may differ from the way you handle a similar one.

Business Class offers a fresh, contemporary approach to creating connections, building solid relationships, increasing your net worth, and getting (and staying) ahead of the competition. It will give you a set of guidelines for treating coworkers, clients, and customers with care, and will prepare you for handling awkward situations or avoiding breaches of etiquette that could tarnish your reputation, sabotage a business deal, or derail your career.

It feels important to share this information with you because whenever you feel a bit insecure or self-conscious in social or business situations, just know that I and many others like you have been there too. And as I am writing this book for you, I am also writing it for myself. Inevitably, I encounter at least one of the scenarios contained in this book each day.

My hope is that in reading this book you will take away some new skills to help you interact more effectively with anyone, anywhere, at any time. Perhaps you will find some difficult moments made easier, and thus you will be able to enhance your visibility, credibility, and profitability.

Before you begin, find out how you fare when it comes to handling some sticky situations in the workplace by taking the following quiz.

test your etiquette intelligence

1. In the business arena
    a. Only men should stand for handshaking and all introductions.
    b. Only women should stand for handshaking and all introductions.
    c. It is not necessary for men or women to stand for handshaking or introductions.
    d. Both men and women should stand for handshaking and all introductions.

2. In the business arena, it is necessary for a man
    a. To pull a chair out for a woman.
    b. To stand when a woman leaves the table.
    c. To pay for a woman's meal.
    d. All of the above.
    e. None of the above.

3. For easy reading, one's name badge should be worn
    a. On the left shoulder.
    b. On the right shoulder.
    c. On the left hip.
    d. Around one's neck.

4. The best way to meet people at a business or social function is to
    a. Head for the bar or the buffet immediately upon arrival.
    b. Introduce yourself to two people who are standing close and talking softly.
    c. Look confident, stand in the center of the room, and wait for someone interesting to approach you.
    d. Introduce yourself to a person standing alone or to large groups.
    e. Stick close to those you know very well and forget about the rest.

5. If you receive an e-mail from an unknown source and realize it should be handled by someone else, you
    a. Forward it immediately.

    b. Forward it with a note explaining why you are sending it.

    c. Consider it spam, delete it, and forget about it.

    d. Print it out and leave it sitting on the copy machine in the hope that someone else will take care of it.

6. If an angry customer calls to complain, you should

    a. Put the person on hold as quickly as possible and blow off some steam in the restroom.

    b. Tell the caller that he has the wrong number and hang up in self-defense.

    c. Stay calm, listen to the caller's complaint, and quickly attempt to help or get help for him.

    d. Quickly put the caller in his place by yelling back. After all, no one has the right to talk to you that way.

7. If you have to introduce two people and you can't remember one person's name, you recover by saying

    a. "Do you know one another?"

    b. "I can't remember your name. Will you introduce yourself?"

    c. Nothing and hoping they will introduce themselves.

    d. "It's been one of those days. Please tell me your name again."

    e. Nothing and doing nothing. After all, you don't want to embarrass yourself or others.

8. When making a business introduction, you

    a. Wing it.

    b. Introduce a client to the president of your company.

    c. Introduce the president of your company to a client.

    d. Don't do anything. It is their responsibility to introduce themselves to one another.

9. After a meeting with a client or vendor, you

    a. Tell her, "Don't call us, we'll call you."

    b. Accompany her to the reception area or elevator.

c. Give her a handshake and a big hug and tell her that you can't wait to see her again.

10. When expressing thanks to someone who has given you a gift, you
    a. Send an e-mail because it is faster and more efficient.
    b. Send a handwritten note.
    c. Pick up the phone and call within seventy-two hours.
    d. Consider a verbal thank you enough.

11. When you are dining with someone important and your cell phone rings, you
    a. Answer it within two rings and keep the call brief.
    b. Ignore it and pretend someone else's phone is ringing.
    c. Apologize and turn the phone on silent mode. The person you're with takes priority.
    d. Apologize, step away from the table, and take the call in the restroom.

12. When you are dining in a restaurant and you accidentally drop your fork on the floor, you
    a. Pick it up, wipe it off, and use it anyway.
    b. Pick it up, give it to the server, and ask him to bring you another one.
    c. Leave it on the floor and ask the server to bring you another one.
    d. Leave it on the floor and use your neighbor's fork while he's not looking.

13. At dinner, when you notice the person on your left eating the roll from your bread plate, you
    a. Tell him he made a mistake and then ask for your roll back.
    b. Don't say anything and eat the roll from your other neighbor's plate.
    c. Don't say anything and try to convince yourself that you didn't need that roll anyway.

    d. Ask the server for another roll and use the side of your dinner plate.

14. If you are carrying a small handbag, you may place it on
    a. A desk.
    b. The back of a chair.
    c. The restaurant table.
    d. None of the above.
    e. Any of the above.

15. At lunch, you notice that the stranger seated next to you has spinach in her teeth, you
    a. Don't say anything, smile, and look her directly in the eye.
    b. Say something and hope you don't embarrass her.
    c. Make visual signals indicating that she has something in her teeth.
    d. Wipe your teeth with your napkin and hope she gets the hint and does the same.

16. If you have a morsel of food lodged in your teeth and you want to remove it, you
    a. Take your knife when no one is looking and remove the morsel promptly with the blade.
    b. Raise your napkin to your mouth and discreetly use a sugar packet or your business card to remove the morsel.
    c. Politely ask your server for a toothpick.
    d. Excuse yourself and go to the restroom to pick your teeth in private.

17. When you bite into a piece of meat that is tough and very difficult to chew, you
    a. Pretend to wipe your mouth and deposit the piece of meat in your napkin.

b. When no one is looking, discreetly use two fingers to remove it and place it on the edge of your plate or underneath a piece of parsley.

c. Swallow it and hope you don't choke.

18. When you take a bite of something very spicy and you notice your nose beginning to run, you
   a. Pull out your handkerchief and gently blot your nose.
   b. Comment on how spicy the food is and use your dinner napkin to blow your nose.
   c. Excuse yourself and go to the restroom.

19. While traveling internationally, you are invited to dinner in someone's home. The host serves a local delicacy that you wouldn't dream of eating in your native country. You
   a. Politely decline by saying "No, thank you" and ask for something else.
   b. Pick at the delicacy with your fork and drink a lot of wine.
   c. Try it and eat as much as you can.
   d. Eat it but let the host know that you are doing it to please him.

20. When you are a guest at a dinner party and the host makes a toast in your honor, you
   a. Show your appreciation by picking up your glass and drinking to yourself.
   b. Leave your glass alone and don't drink to yourself.
   c. Don't drink because you don't like cheap champagne.
   d. Get embarrassed and tell your host you don't deserve the recognition.

21. When you are finished eating, your napkin should be
   a. Folded loosely and placed on the right side of the plate.
   b. Folded loosely and placed on the left side of the plate.
   c. Folded loosely and placed in the center of the plate.

d. Folded like a dove or a pirate's hat and placed on the seat of your chair.

etiquette quiz answers

1. d	7. d	13. d or c	19. c
2. e	8. c	14. d	20. b
3. b	9. b	15. a	21. b
4. d	10. b	16. d	
5. b	11. c	17. b	
6. c	12. c	18. a	

First, and Lasting, Impressions

It takes twenty years to build a reputation and five minutes to ruin it. If you think about that, you'll do things differently.

—Warren Buffett,
stock market investor and
business tycoon

hoever said "You never get a second chance to make a first impression" was absolutely right. In business and in private life, we either consciously or unconsciously make judgments about someone's professionalism, character, and competence based on first impressions. The best way to make a positive first impression, especially during first-time business encounters, is to be on time and be prepared.

Uncommon Common Sense

- *Give a firm handshake.*
- *Say "Please," "Thank you," and "Excuse me."*
- *Don't interrupt or finish a person's sentence.*
- *Return phone calls promptly.*
- *Be punctual.*

P. M. Forni, author of *Choosing Civility: The Twenty-five Rules of Considerate Conduct* and cofounder of the Johns Hopkins Civility Project, says that one of the reasons we experience stress in business encounters is lack of preparation. "It's like an exam. If you have studied for the exam, you will be less nervous and will show authority and poise," says Forni. He believes that when you are prepared, you think more clearly. Instead of investing nervous energy in anticipating the situation, you invest that energy in thinking about the problems and issues at hand. Pre-meeting preparation will give you an enormous advantage over someone else who shows up without having done their homework. James R. Lucas, president and CEO of Luman Consultants International, a management consulting company in Overland Park, Kansas, and author of *Fatal Illusions: Shredding a Dozen Unrealities That Can Keep Your Organization from Success,* believes you set yourself up for failure when you don't take the time to learn anything about your client or vendor. In a recent phone interview, Lucas told me, "Learn everything you can about your clients. Each one is uniquely different and each has their own special needs. Don't try to use a one-size-fits-all approach. Customizing builds memorable relationships."

During one of my etiquette seminars, an attorney told me he prepares for a business meeting the same way he prepares for a trial. In preparing for a trial, he researches the evidence, interviews suspects or witnesses, and finds out as much as possible before presenting his case. Before meeting with a client or his law partners, his preparation is similar. If you spend the time it takes to glean important background information, you can be better prepared for your next client meeting or job interview by doing the following:

- Find out who you will be meeting. Memorize the names and titles of those you don't know. During the meeting, use each person's name several times in conversation.
- Visit their Web site to view the company's history, mission statement, staff biographies, articles, news releases, and more. Take notes on index cards and review them just before the meeting. This research is also good fodder for conversation.
- Break the ice by discussing topics that interest those who are attending the meeting. Aside from the weather and traffic, most people feel comfortable talking about their alma mater, hobbies, special interests, and vacations. If you don't know what interests the person outside of work, ask a colleague who knows him well. If you share something in common, like running in marathons, make mention of it.
- Familiarize yourself with the industry in which you'll be working. Read trade publications and get acquainted with the acronyms, buzzwords, trends, and the client's competitors' problems or issues.
- Brush up on current events by reading weekly newsmagazines and one or two major daily newspapers. You'll appear more interesting and knowledgeable if you're apprised of what's going on in the world.

A strategy is equally important when you attend internal meetings with your boss or coworkers. To prepare:

- Read over the meeting agenda and support material and familiarize yourself with the topics to be discussed. Suggest any modifications to the agenda before the meeting begins.
- If you're unable to attend a meeting, send someone in your absence.
- If you're chairing the meeting, make sure everyone contributes to the conversation.

- Discourage sidebar conversations.
- Jot down any pertinent questions or issues you want to address. The worst thing you can do is go to a meeting and say nothing.
- If you're chairing the meeting, make a "call to action" list and document who is going to follow up on certain tasks. Assign deadlines for each task.
- Distribute meeting minutes within twenty-four hours.

BEFRIEND THE GATEKEEPER

First impressions begin as soon as you arrive at someone's office, so it's best to be friendly to the receptionist or whoever greets you as you walk in, or when you stop by to drop off information or arrive to meet someone. In a survey commissioned by Robert Half International, 91 percent of executives polled said they consider the opinions of their executive assistants when it comes to hiring someone for a job or making certain business decisions. Anyone who is rude or indifferent to a receptionist or executive assistant (or anyone else in the company) can sacrifice their chances of getting a foot in the door.

Linda Kaplan Thaler, CEO and CCO (chief creative officer) of the Kaplan Thaler Group, an advertising agency in New York City and coauthor of *BANG!: Getting Your Message Heard in a Noisy World,* says if a business candidate treats her executive assistant poorly, she refuses to do business with that person. One day while Kaplan Thaler was interviewing a job candidate, her executive assistant, Fran, brought the candidate a cup of coffee. "I thanked my assistant for getting the applicant's cup of coffee but the applicant just looked at her and kept on talking to me," says Kaplan Thaler. "At that moment I decided not to hire this person. When he didn't thank her, I got a complete snapshot of his character. It's the small things that define someone's true personality," she explains. "If you break a mirror into a million pieces, you can pick up one sliver and still get his or her whole character reflection."

Eva Rosenberg, publisher of TaxMama.com, a tax information Web site, agrees with Kaplan Thaler. She says it's a mistake to assume the gatekeeper has no decision-making power. "If you're a sales rep who calls my assistant and you are rude to her, you've already lost the sale. She's going to say to me, 'This guy's a jerk,' and I'm going to take her word for it. I always rely on her to tell me which calls are important. In fact, many times, she has the authority to make purchases on her own," says Rosenberg.

C. Leslie Charles, founder of TRAININGWORKS, a human resources development firm in East Lansing, Michigan, and author of *Why Is Everyone So Cranky?: The Ten Trends Complicating Our Lives and What We Can Do About Them,* recalls the time when she worked with a copy machine sales representative who ruined his chances for a sale because he let his ego get in the way. While Charles was a job trainee shadowing a sales rep, she saw him trying to go over the secretary's head to get to the president of the company. "He thought he was a hotshot and treated the administrative assistant as if she didn't know a thing about copy machines. In the end, the president of the company let the secretary choose the copy machine because she was the primary user. Needless to say, Mr. Hotshot didn't make the cut due to his poor judgment and bad manners," says Charles.

Here are some ways to win points with an executive assistant:

- When you meet an executive assistant, shake his hand and acknowledge him by name if you know it.

- If you are offered a cup of coffee or a glass of water, accept it graciously. This is a great time to start a brief conversation.
- While waiting for your meeting, engage in some small talk with the executive assistant. This will help establish a rapport, as long as you are not distracting her from her work. Comment on pictures of her children or a nice pin or scarf she may be wearing. When all else fails, talk about the weather.
- During the holidays, go the extra mile and bring a small gift, like a box of chocolates, to the executive assistant. You will be remembered for your thoughtfulness and you will have something to talk about the next time you call or visit. (Some companies have strict policies on gifts, so research the limitations ahead of time.)
- Thank the executive assistant by name when you leave.
- During follow-up phone calls, use the executive assistant's name in conversation and exchange pleasantries before asking to speak with the president or CEO. For example, say something like, "Hello Chris, this is Ken Hines. Did you have a nice vacation?"

DURING THE MEETING: MEASURE THE MOOD

Food lovers have been known to travel hours to the world-famous Inn at Little Washington for a taste of chef Patrick O'Connell's grilled black figs with tangy lime sauce, a medallion of veal tenderloin with woodsy mushrooms, or a slice of Valrhona chocolate cake with roasted-banana ice cream. While the food is delectable, it's the attention to detail that takes the dining experience over the top.

Chef O'Connell believes that people aren't impressed by what you know or what you can offer until they see that you care. He believes you can't possibly care in any meaningful way unless you have some insight into what people are feeling and why. Staffers in the one-hundred-seat dining room are apprised of a guest's "mood rating" upon arrival. Using a scale of 1 to 10, with 7 or below indicating displeasure or unhappiness, the captain secretly assigns to each table a number that corresponds to the guests' apparent state of mind. The mood rating is typed into a computer, written on the dinner order, and placed on a spool in the kitchen where the entire staff can see it and react accordingly. "If guests ran into terrible traffic on the way here, or are in the midst of a marital dispute, we need to consider it our problem. How else are we going to ensure that they have a sublime experience?" muses O'Connell.

In business the ability to measure a client's or colleague's mood is even more invaluable if you want to get a business discussion off to a good start either on the phone or in person. First determine whether the person you're meeting with wants to socialize or would rather get down to business right away. Some people want to jump straight into a discussion, while others want to ask about your family, vacation, or other personal matters before talking shop. If someone is cheerful and wants to small-talk before getting to business matters, then you do the same. If someone walks in the door and is eager to discuss business, then happily follow along. Although chitchat is an important part of building relationships, it might not be expected or encouraged when attending a meeting, so follow the lead of the person in charge.

SLOW DOWN: MAKE FRIENDS

Regardless of whether a meeting is held at or away from your office, the first few minutes will generally involve some chitchat.

This is a good time to establish rapport. If you are meeting with someone new, glance around their office as you walk in and look for indicators of personal interests. Like one's home, an office often reflects one's personality. Personal items on the desk or wall, particularly pictures of family, pets, or sports, are fodder for conversation. If you notice any plaques, diplomas, or personal or professional awards, comment on them. Everyone loves recognition and genuine praise. When you establish rapport, you gain a friendship. When you gain a friendship, you increase your chances of gaining a job, a referral, a recommendation, a promotion, or a long-term contract.

AFTER THE MEETING: DEFINE GOALS AND EXPECTATIONS

At the end of a meeting, ask questions and then summarize the person's concerns and expectatons and share ways in which you can help summarize goals, responsibilities, and deadlines in writing. Follow up when you say you're going to follow up. Underpromise and overdeliver, and deliver on time or even sooner. If your client or coworker has expectations you can't fulfill, explain what you can realistically provide. If there's something you aren't able to accomplish by yourself, recommend others who may be able to help. Maintain a stellar professional reputation. It may take years to gain someone's respect but it takes only seconds to lose it.

TIPS FROM THE TOP

Find out what you can about a person before an important meeting.

Be extra nice to the executive assistant.

Establish rapport before getting down to business.

Build a friendship and the sale will eventually follow.

Don't promise more than you can deliver.

Chapter 2

Small Touches Equal Big Business

> Small kindnesses, small courtesies, small considera-
> tions, habitually practiced in our social intercourse,
> give a greater charm to the character than the display
> of great talents and accomplishments.
>
> —Mary Ann Kelty,
> *British author*

When my husband and I renovated our home several years ago, we decided to install an alarm system. It was my assignment to call three reputable companies and ask for a price quote. Although price was important, it wasn't the deciding factor. A large part of my decision was based on the way one sales representative, Edward Abrahams, made me feel. If I had to pinpoint one particular thing I liked about Edward, I couldn't do it. It was a combination of many small, yet important, factors. I liked the way he quickly responded to my phone calls, the professional way he presented himself and his product, the way he looked me in the eye, shook my hand, and intelligently answered my long list of questions. Most of all, I liked how he took the time to make me feel as if I were his only customer. Twenty or thirty years ago, this kind of service might have been customary; today it is extraordinary. These small things added up and gave Edward an advantage over his competitors.

A common admonition in life and in business is "Don't sweat the small stuff." Yet if you ignore the small stuff, better known as common courtesies, you could lose current clients—the ones who mysteriously disappear without ever saying a word—or lose the respect and support of colleagues. Minor irritants, random acts of rudeness, or unconscious brush-offs make us want to avoid doing business with someone.

If you offend a client, the financial pinch might not be felt immediately but eventually it takes its toll. It costs 500 percent more to attract a new customer than to retain a current one, according to *The One to One Future* by Don Peppers and Martha Rogers. Put simply, small courtesies make for big sales. Imagine owning or working for a dry cleaning business and having a customer who spends $5 every week for fifty-two weeks to get her shirts washed and pressed. If you, or one of your employees or coworkers, have a bad day and say something to offend your customer, she will probably go somewhere else if an apology is not offered, even if it means driving several miles out of her way. As a result of your customer's disappointment, your company would lose $260 in annual revenues. Multiply that by the number of customers who go away unhappy and the numbers quickly become significant.

Because we live in a fast-paced, often impersonal era, it's more critical than ever to offer the little niceties that might easily be forgotten, yet make others feel important or appreciated. Little things, such as smiling and cheerfully greeting a coworker, remembering a client's name or his children's names, or asking about someone's ailing friend or family member, establishes a rapport that eventually leads to stronger business relationships. Forgetting to return an important phone call, taking too long to acknowledge or respond to someone's request, neglecting to thank someone who helped you complete a project, or forgetting to do something you said you were going to do has the potential to diminish your credibility with colleagues or wreak financial havoc with clients.

A GOOD BRAND IS NOT ENOUGH

A good reputation, a well-known name, and a prominent address are advantageous in business but are not enough to attract and keep employees and clients happy. Jeffrey Fox, CEO of Fox & Company, a marketing consulting company, and best-selling author of *How to Become a Rainmaker: The Rules for Getting and Keeping Customers and Clients,* says he once had a boss who used to say that if your office was located in a desirable spot like Fifth Avenue in New York City, you'd never have to worry about dissatisfied customers. "In today's world, that is no longer the case," says Fox. "If you can't satisfy your customers in New York City, or anywhere else for that matter, you'll be out of business in no time flat." In the workplace, generous pay and a hefty benefits package don't make up for failure to treat employees well or acknowledge them for a job well done. In the end, they will eventually seek other employment opportunities, thus costing your company thousands of dollars to recruit and train a new hire.

In today's competitive business arena, just about anyone can match or beat prices and everyone promises great service. But if you want to attract and keep customers and employees, you have to offer something different, something that distinguishes you from the crowd. It's the small touches, like practicing good business etiquette, that will set you apart and make it practically impossible to be derailed by competitors. Keep the lines of communication open by encouraging clients and coworkers to share new ideas, solicit positive feedback and constructive criticism, and never berate or demoralize a client or coworker in public. The ability to get along with people is an asset beyond price. It is a shortcut to success.

The following are some simple, yet forgotten, business principles that win relationships and keep your credibility intact whether you're self-employed or you work for a small or large company.

Be honest. Unfortunately, the business world has been rocked by fraud and scandals in recent years, and chances are, more will be unearthed in the future. Your credibility is based on your ability to be honest in all situations. You well know that you could potentially damage your career, lose your job, and ruin your reputation if you were to intentionally lie, or misstate or misrepresent yourself or your products or services. The truth may occasionally hurt, but dishonesty is always destructive.

Keep your word. Every day you have the opportunity to either raise or lower your credibility quotient when you make promises. You know the importance of being upfront and letting your clients, associates, or colleagues know what to expect before starting any new project. You'll want to keep all those involved apprised of any changes that directly impact your department, your company, or someone else's company. If you can't complete a task on time or stay within the agreed-upon budget, notify your clients or coworkers immediately. No one likes surprises unless they're an absolute plus. If things go wrong, people tend to be more forgiving when they've been forewarned. You will become brighter in your client's or boss's eyes every time you meet a deadline, fulfill a request, complete a task, or keep a promise. As you know, your word is all you've got. Nothing is gained by withholding critical information, and your professional credibility decays when you don't deliver on your promises.

Admit mistakes. Dr. Joyce Brothers was right when she said "The person interested in success has to learn to view failure as a healthy, inevitable part of the process of getting to the top." It's not the mistakes but the way in which we handle them that will make or break our reputation. Don't try to cover up, ignore, or minimize your or your company's blunders. This will only compound things. Mistakes will happen, so it's best to own up to them, learn from them, then move on.

Stacy Allison, motivational speaker and the first American woman to reach the summit of Mount Everest, says blame slows us down. "Don't try to cover mistakes up and don't blame others. Take responsibility and correct mistakes as soon as possible. Usually people are more forgiving when you are up-front and fix them expeditiously," says Allison. Success comes when you focus on the solutions rather than dwelling on the problems.

Be punctual. Arriving on time is less impressive than being a few minutes early. Arriving early means you have the opportunity to go to the restroom, check your appearance, and gain your composure before starting your workday or attending an important meeting. Always allow extra time to account for traffic delays, inclement weather, or parking problems.

If you do find yourself running late, call ahead to say you are on your way. Make sure being late is an exception. When you are repeatedly late you lose your credibility by sending a signal that you don't respect others' time. Avoid making up lame excuses. Should you find yourself arriving late due to unforeseen circumstances, simply apologize and say no more.

Choose your words carefully. Another's impression of you is partially the result of what you say and how you say it. According to a study conducted for American Demographics by the market research firm Harris Interactive, sixty-three percent of Americans say they swear in public, but doing so can work against you. Using profanity and foul language in public may give others the impression that you are immature, impatient, and lacking in self-control. Besides, the use of "colorful" language doesn't command respect or admiration. It can, however, make others feel uncomfortable. Improper language gives clients a good reason to take their business elsewhere and gives coworkers a reason to not want to work with you. It's not worth the risk of alienating yourself from others. When you're angry or upset, walk away to avoid letting any harsh words roll off your tongue and into the wrong ears.

Handle conflict with grace. The potential for arguments and disagreements is always going to be a part of doing business with others. There will be times when you have a disagreement or lose an argument. However, it's how you handle an awkward or tempestuous situation that will reveal your character. Do you yield with grace when you or your company is in the wrong, or do you get angry and take your frustrations out on your customers and coworkers? Gary Aldrich, president and founder of the Patrick Henry Center for Individual Liberty, a nonprofit foundation dedicated to promoting the U.S. Constitution and Bill of Rights, once told me, "No one leads a perfect life where you always win a perfect battle. When you learn to live with setbacks, you achieve a certain grace." You're bound to encounter clients, customers, and coworkers who test your patience or question your abilities or authority. In times of conflict and adversity, the strongest leaders don't get ruffled easily. When you're boiling inside, never let others see you come unglued. People will be receptive to working with you if you can maintain a calm, unwavering demeanor in the best and worst of situations.

Don't burn bridges. It was a cold day in January 1992, figuratively and physically, when I received a call from the director of recreation summoning me to her office. What I thought was going to be another meeting turned out to be a conversation regarding a department-wide layoff. After I lost my job, I continued to stay in touch with my director. Two years after being let go, she was happy to give me a good reference when I interviewed for the public relations position at the Breakers Hotel in Palm Beach. Her glowing recommendation helped me get the job.

Although losing my job was tough to endure at the time, the experience taught me three important lessons about life. Never become complacent and assume that because you're doing a great job, nothing can happen to you, because something can. Never speak negatively about a past employer or business relationship that turns sour. And don't burn any bridges—your adversary today could be your ally tomorrow.

Practice these virtues and let them guide you in doing business with others. While arriving on time, being honest, and returning phone calls may seem like small pieces of the puzzle, when they are all put together, they add up to the big picture you project of yourself—one that conveys that you are poised, polished, and ready to interact with others in the highest professional manner.

TIPS FROM THE TOP

Be honest and admit when you're wrong.

Arrive early, not just on time.

Refrain from foul language.

Speak favorably of past employers and clients.

Chapter 3

Suit Up For Success

Clothes and manners do not make the man; but, when
he is made, they greatly improve his appearance.

—Henry Ward Beecher,
American clergyman, orator,
and lecturer

I am married to a type-A personality. My husband,
Brian, is a perfectionist in everything he does, and during his downtime he enjoys working in the garden. I've never seen
anyone with a greener thumb. He can take a dead plant, put it in a
pot of dirt, give it some water, and weeks later it will miraculously
spring back to life.

Each little plant, tree, and flower in our garden looks perfectly
groomed because Brian spends the time and effort to keep everything looking lush, healthy, and well manicured. These little landscaping details—flowers and greenery—make a big difference in
enhancing a home's outside appearance. In the world of real estate, brokers and agents know it's easier to sell a house that has attractive landscaping. They call it "curb appeal." If the outside of a

house is pretty and well maintained, buyers are more curious to look at the inside.

In business, people too need curb appeal. If your outward appearance is neat and attractive, people will want to know more about what you offer on the inside. What we wear says a lot about who we are and where we want to be. Professor P. M. Forni of Johns Hopkins University says, "When we dress professionally and formally, we make a statement that says, I want to be respected, and I want to be taken seriously."

We've all been told that our appearance speaks louder than words. The following are some other advantages to looking good.

A nice appearance enhances your personal brand. Joe Vitale, author of *The Attractor Factor: 5 Easy Steps for Creating Wealth (Or Anything Else.) From the Inside Out*, believes we develop our perceptions based on what we see. "When others look at the way you dress, they make conclusions about you. Every time you dress well, you positively influence the way you're perceived," says Vitale.

Part of the Walt Disney Company's success is attributed to its notorious dress code. Beginning in 1955, Walt Disney insisted that all of his employees have a clean-cut, all-American image. To this day, the "Disney look" has been emulated by hundreds of companies. Gayle Treutel, former appearance specialist for the Walt Disney World Company, says that until about fifteen years ago, female cast members could not wear colored panty hose, bright nail polish, dark lipstick, or heavy makeup. Earrings could be no larger than a penny and hair had to be neatly trimmed and pulled away from the face. The men had to be clean-shaven and their hair couldn't touch their collar. The Disney dress code has become more elastic in recent years but is still more stringent than most. Take it from Walt Disney, if you want to heighten your company's level of professionalism, implement a dress code.

A nice appearance enhances your overall package. Like gift wrapping, the more "put together" your appearance, the more you will leave a positive impression. Michael Levine, founder of the public relations firm Levine Communications Office in Los Angeles and author of *Guerilla P.R.: How You Can Wage an Effective Publicity Campaign—Without Going Broke*, calls this the "Tiffany Theory." According to Levine, if you give someone a present in a blue Tiffany box, it's likely they'll perceive the gift to have a higher value than if it is presented without a box or in a box with less prestige. Levine says we live in a culture in which we gift wrap everything—politicians, corporate executives, sports stars, actors, and news anchors. Whether we are interviewing for a job, asking for a promotion, or soliciting a new account, he believes, people buy our entire package, and the way we dress is a major part of that package. Successful people know the value of packaging with a purpose.

U.S. Representative Mark Foley told me he believes a person's appearance can either make or break one's total image. "You don't have to wear a designer suit, but pay attention to the basics. Make sure that your clothes are clean and pressed, your shoes are polished, your hair is combed, and your nails are neat. If you take the time to put some thought and effort in your appearance, you will set yourself head and shoulders above your competition," says Foley.

A nice appearance pays big dividends. If you ever walk into a store on Rodeo Drive in Beverly Hills or on Worth Avenue in Palm Beach, you will undoubtedly be greeted by a sales associate who is impeccably dressed from head to toe. After all, if you're going to pay a few thousand dollars for a Chanel or Armani suit, wouldn't you want to buy it from someone who looks as sharp as the suit itself? Although details such as exquisite fabric, bias cuts, and hand-sewing contribute to the suit's high cost, many well-known designers believe that if the cost of their products is high, then their designs will have a greater value. In our society, there's an appearance perception: dressing well equates success. Research shows that employers are willing to pay higher salaries to well-dressed applicants. Judith Walters of Fairleigh Dickinson University researched the connection between an effective business appearance and starting salaries. She sent out a group of identical résumés to more than a thousand companies. Some of the résumés were accompanied by a "before makeover" photo of an applicant, others by an "after makeover" photo. Each company was asked to determine a starting salary. Starting salaries ranged 8 to 20 percent higher as the result of upgrading a mediocre appearance to one that was polished and professional.

A nice appearance gets your foot in the door. Research shows that the number one reason companies reject an applicant after the first interview is poor personal appearance. Barbara Corcoran, founder and chairman of the Corcoran Group, New York's leading residential real estate company, says many of her company's hiring decisions are based on first impressions. She has four pet peeves: when someone comes in for an interview wearing rugged, outdoor-type sandals; wears too much perfume or aftershave; doesn't stand up to shake hands; or acts too casually. "We're a Madison Avenue firm, so we expect our applicants to present themselves in the highest professional manner possible," says Corcoran. "When someone wears inappropriate attire or has bathed in cologne, it shows poor judgment. If the potential employee comes in projecting an image of professionalism, that's one less thing our firm has to worry about."

Corcoran says body language also plays a part in a person's overall appearance. "We've seen applicants who put their elbows or briefcases on our desk. Others slouch in their chair; if you're leaning back, it sends a signal that you're not as interested in a job as you should be," says Corcoran. These red flags are not always the deciding factor as to whether or not a person gets a job, but Corcoran says they certainly don't help matters much. "If someone is dressed well, it doesn't necessarily mean they are qualified for the job, but if their appearance is inappropriate, they don't get to second base," says Corcoran. Be aware of a company's dress code policy before you conduct business or interview for a job. In general it's better to err on the formal side rather than to be underdressed. Keep a jacket or blazer in your car or on the back of your door in the event the occasion calls for an important meeting with someone.

When she started her company in 1951, Lillian Vernon, founder of the Lillian Vernon Corporation, says the rules for business attire were not as complex then as they are today. That's why she advocates being overdressed versus underdressed, especially when interviewing for a job. She said she doesn't hire anyone who is dressed sloppily or inappropriately for an interview. Vernon believes that if a job is important to someone, they should demonstrate their desire by dressing well. "If you wear sloppy or inappropriate attire, it says you don't respect yourself and won't care how you reflect on the company," says Vernon. "Presenting a professional, appropriate image says that you are prepared and promotable."

LOOK THE PART

If you want a position in a bank, look like a banker. If you want to work at a hair salon, look like a stylist. In my case, I had to look like a flight attendant. After my position at the Walt Disney World Dolphin was eliminated, I interviewed for a job with Northwest Airlines. Northwest was conducting a nationwide search for flight attendants and the recruiters were coming to my hometown. A couple of days before the interview, I called Northwest, spoke with someone in reservations, and asked her a series of questions about the company and its history. I also asked how flight attendants dressed.

The day of my interview I showed up, as did three hundred other applicants, but you could have picked me out of the crowd because I was the only one who looked like a flight attendant. I wore a dark blue skirt with a matching jacket, a collared white shirt, dark hose, and navy pumps. During the selection process, each applicant was asked to stand in front of the audience and for one minute talk about why she or he wanted to work for the company. The next day, I received a much-anticipated phone call from the recruiting manager inviting me back for a second interview. That interview went so well, I was hired on the spot. Only three applicants were chosen that day, and I am convinced that one of the reasons the interviewers chose me was because I looked the part. Clothes can either detract from or enhance a person's appearance. When doing business with someone, especially during negotiations, choose a subtle outfit that enhances your appearance while allowing your intelligence and talents to shine.

CORPORATE CASUAL SPELLS COSTLY CHAOS

When you have an appointment with a doctor, lawyer, or financial advisor, do you expect the person to be dressed a certain way? I'm sure the last thing you want is for a licensed professional to be casual about your needs, indifferent about your time, and dressed as if he or she is ready for a game of golf or a workout at the gym. The way we dress for work or for a meeting should not be any different. "Business casual" has made its way into the corporate arena and has caused a great deal of confusion. Some employers tell me they have trouble defining their dress code and communicating their expectations, and their employees have trouble interpreting them. Jeffrey Fox of Fox & Company says being in business is not a casual affair. He says dressing well projects self-respect and shows that you respect those you're with on any given day.

If you're a manager or CEO, you can't be upset with an employee if they aren't dressing according to your expectations, especially if you don't clearly define exactly what you want them to wear. It's important to put company dress code guidelines in writing. "Informality gives people the impression that there are no rules, and people get in trouble when boundaries are unclear," says P. M. Forni. William Mahoney, president and CEO of Mahoney & Associates, an executive compensation and benefits management firm in Fort Lauderdale, Florida, and Springfield, Massachusetts, makes his company's appearance guidelines crystal clear to his employees after they are hired. "Any modifications to the corporate dress code are not tolerated," says Mahoney.

If your company or your client's company observes a "business casual" dress code, find out what level is most appropriate and dress accordingly. "Business casual" has various levels of casualness for women and men. For example, a man may find that a pair of khaki pants worn with a cotton polo shirt is appropriate for an off-site meeting with a high-tech company, whereas a long-sleeved dress shirt, a blazer, and a pair of dark, wool gabardine trousers would be appropriate for an off-site meeting with a restaurant owner. A woman may wear khakis and a long-sleeved cotton shirt, or a wool skirt and a cashmere twin set, or a pair of tweed pants and a blazer, depending on the situation and corporate culture. When you're not sure what is appropriate, notice how the person above you on the corporate ladder dresses. If you are self-employed, dress on the higher end. Men should never leave their office or home without a jacket and tie. If you find yourself in an informal setting you can always leave your jacket in your car or take your tie off when you arrive.

Graeme Black, Ferragamo's head designer, reports, "People used to talk about dressing more casually in the office, but that hasn't really worked out. People need to look a certain way to command authority." Fashion faux pas can kill your credibility.

Details Complete a Wardrobe

Sometimes the little touches make the biggest impact. Accessories are small luxuries that create a favorable impression. The following are a few suggestions about key accessories that add to your overall professional image.

Carry a quality pen. As special events manager for the Walt Disney World Dolphin, I would attend weekly preconference

Fashion Faux Pas at Work

- *Exercise clothes*
- *Tennis attire*
- *Beachwear*
- *Short shorts*
- *Gardening clothes*
- *Nightclub attire*
- *Miniskirts (shorter than two inches above the knee)*
- *Rhinestone-studded or torn jeans*
- *Souvenir/logo T-shirts*
- *Revealing blouses*
- *Crop tops*
- *Sweatshirts, sweatpants, or leggings*
- *Sneakers*
- *Flip-flops*
- *Stiletto heels*
- *Scuffed shoes with worn heels or tattered soles*
- *Heavy perfume or cologne*
- *Stained or wrinkled clothes*
- *Panty hose with open-toed shoes*
- *Wet hair*
- *Excessive jewelry*

meetings with meeting planners who were bringing their groups to the hotel. As I sat in the meetings, I couldn't help but notice the catering manager's designer fountain pen with a black lacquer finish. Although it seems small, it had a big effect on the way I perceived his overall image. Everything about him was nicely put together, his suit, tie, and hair, but that fountain pen completed his impeccable appearance. You don't have to spend a lot of money on a pen, but it should look attractive and write well.

Invest in a few good suits. Each time you get dressed, you are making a powerful statement about yourself. People unconsciously form judgments about your background, socioeconomic status, level of education, and personality traits based on what you're wearing. If you underdress, you may embarrass yourself or others; if you overdress, you may intimidate or set the wrong tone. That's why it's important to know how to dress for any occasion.

Wear clothing that reflects the level you wish to achieve rather than the level on which you're currently working.

Lou Amendola, vice president of merchandising for Brooks Brothers, says the pendulum is moving toward a more formal way of dressing. He says, "Over the past two years, business casual has been receding. The style is changing back to people dressing up at work again." You may not be required to wear or feel like wearing a suit every day, but there will be times when dressing more formally will be appropriate and perhaps expected. A suit is your best bet when you have a big presentation, performance evaluation, important sales meeting, or lunch with your boss or another department head. When you put on a suit, you assume the role that comes with it. You will find that you walk a little taller and have more confidence. Whenever you wear a suit you give the impression that you're serious about the business at hand.

Buy quality, not quantity. In his book *Trump: How to Get Rich,* Donald Trump says that he used to pride himself on buying very inexpensive suits and other clothing until he realized that good quality items don't wear out as fast. "I now buy high-quality shoes, and they seem to last forever, whereas the cheap ones used to wear out quickly and always looked as cheap as the price I'd paid for them."

Both men and women should purchase good quality "global" clothing, especially for business travel. Select lightweight, breathable fabrics that don't wrinkle easily and can be worn in multiple climates. It will be more cost-efficient in the long run if you purchase suits made from fabrics such as wool or a wool blend that can be worn successfully to a meeting in San Francisco and still look appropriate in New York, London, or Hong Kong. Colors such as black, navy, taupe, and charcoal are professional, travel well, and don't look seasonal. A woman may show her individuality with accessories like scarves, handbags, and high-quality jewelry and a man may show his with a variety of silk ties.

Beware of bulky baggage. Sometimes it doesn't matter how well dressed you are if your accessories look shabby and worn. Mary Lou Andre, president of Organization By Design, a wardrobe management and fashion consulting firm in Needham, Massachusetts, and author of *Ready to Wear: An Expert's Guide to Choosing and Using Your Wardrobe*, says it's important to take good care of your handbags and briefcases so they don't detract from your overall image. "Someone who walks into a meeting toting a scuffed, bulging briefcase is going to appear harried and disorganized, no matter how well dressed," says Andre. She believes in keeping your bag neat and orderly. "A bag overstuffed with papers can give people the impression that you are disorganized and sloppy," she says. "Your handbag or briefcase does more than just hold important papers, a wallet, and a cell phone. It holds clues about your success, professionalism, and personality." Think "classic and timeless" when purchasing important accessories and they will serve you for years without ever going out of style.

Put your best foot forward. Shoes say a lot about who we are. Aerosoles senior vice president Kimberley Grayson says she always looks at feet first to see how pulled-together a person is. Shoes should be in good condition, not tired, dusty, and worn. Shoes are your most important accessory because they do more than simply complete your ensemble; good-looking, polished shoes help convey your professional image and attention to detail. People who take pride in their appearance show that pride in the small details, such as wearing a good-quality pair of shoes. Your feet need to last the rest of your life, so take good care of them by wearing the best shoes you can possibly afford.

Sounding Off: Speak More Professionally

Image is more than the way you act and look; it also reflects the way you speak. How you communicate conveys more than what you say. It doesn't matter what profession you've chosen, if your voice is unpleasant to others, it is a liability. Knowing how to communicate clearly and effectively is a boon to your career.

Lower your pitch. Some executives, particularly women, speak in a high-pitched, childlike voice or use an indecisive-sounding upward pitch (called "upspeak") at the end of statements. Statements begin sounding like questions and cause even the most intelligent and knowledgeable professional to come across as uninformed or insecure. To avoid sounding uncertain, make your voice go down in pitch at the end of your sentences without going down in volume.

Avoid filler words. Some people are uncomfortable with voids in conversation and feel that every second needs to be filled with sounds, words, or phrases such as "like," "um," and "you know what I mean?" Filler words, if used in excess, can be distracting, annoying, and unprofessional.

Park your personal problems at home. Constant complaining and speaking negatively about a client, boss, or coworker can make others in the office feel uneasy. It's best to leave problems such as your relationship troubles, financial woes, or health issues at home.

Accept compliments. When people praise you for a great job or for your nice appearance, accept their remarks with a simple, assertive "Thank you." Don't be shy about giving compliments. There's so little praise in this world. Give it out generously. American author and professor Leo Buscaglia once said, "Too often we underestimate the power of a touch, a smile, a kind word, a listening ear, an honest compliment, or the smallest act of caring, all of which have the potential to turn a life around."

The best part of looking good on the outside is how it makes you feel on the inside. Once you have polished your shoes and polished your look and presentation, you will feel more confident and be ready to shake hands and exchange meaningful small talk in any business interaction.

TIPS FROM THE TOP

Keep your elbows off the boardroom table.

Dress for the job you want, not the job you have.

Wear clothes that look good and travel well.

Invest in a good tailor and dry cleaner.

Speak clearly and avoid filler words.

Accept compliments graciously.

Chapter 4

MASTER YOUR MINGLE-ABILITY

A single conversation with a wise man is better than
ten years of study.

—CHINESE PROVERB

As a child, I spent many afternoons at my grandmother's house while my mother worked at her hair salon. It wasn't unusual for one or two friends to pop in and see Granny Johnson on any given day, but one person in particular used to make monthly visits. He was a tall, jovial man named Mel Barber, an insurance agent with Gulf Life Insurance. Mel would stay about twenty minutes and chat awhile about the weather or whatever TV show Granny might have watched that day. After exchanging pleasantries and drinking a glass of iced tea, Mel would say good-bye until his next visit. Although his sole purpose for stopping in was to collect the monthly insurance payment, it never seemed as if Mel conducted any business. He had an effortless way of putting people at ease and treating them like close friends or family members. Perhaps it was his easygoing disposition that made him so likeable, but Mel knew all about networking long before the word existed.

Mel's way of doing business one-on-one is no longer commonplace. In today's world, executives connect with colleagues, customers, and potential clients en masse at cocktail parties, corporate events, trade shows, and other venues. Connecting at large and small events can be an arduous process if you have difficulty putting on a smile and mingling with a room full of strangers.

According to the Shyness Research Institute at Indiana University Southeast, 88 percent of people report feeling shy at some point. A few months ago I met a woman named Margaret. She confessed to me that she loathed the idea of going to parties with her husband, who is a well-known antique dealer, lamenting that she had nothing in common with his circle of business associates. Like Margaret, many of us, at one time or another, are turned off by the idea of networking with people who have markedly different interests. There are times when I would rather stay at home, curl up on my couch, and watch *Seinfeld* reruns versus getting dressed up and going to another cocktail party.

For some, "networking" conjures up images of overzealous "here's my card, give me a call" hustlers who are intent on selling you something you don't want or need. To others, networking means working your way through a room as if you're being paid by the handshake. Regardless of how you feel about interacting with strangers, networking is undeniably one of the most effective ways of meeting people who can help you grow your career or your business. More important, it's a way for you to help others grow their career or their business.

Practice Makes Perfect

Effective networking requires study and practice before it becomes second nature. P. M. Forni of Johns Hopkins University believes that the more you interact with others, the more comfortable you will feel. "It's like being able to swim. If you approach a body of water and you know how to swim, you will be less nervous," says Professor Forni. "If you cross a border and enter a new country, you will be less nervous if you can speak the language. The more you engage in social interaction, the less anxious you will be. You will have more authority and poise if you know the rules of engagement."

See and Be Seen

The first rule of networking is visibility. In order for people to know who you are, you must see and be seen. Join professional organizations, associations, and other groups that need your talents. Volunteer to serve on boards and committees, and attend charity fund-raising events. Get involved with extracurricular activities at work. Hone your public speaking skills and give presentations at industry association meetings or be a guest lecturer at a community college or a university. If you feel your skills are not up to par, take a public speaking class at a local college or university or contact Toastmasters (*www.toastmasters.org*) and find information about clubs in your area. If you already speak professionally, the National Speakers Association (*www.nsaspeaker.org*) provides resources and educational opportunities that will help take your speaking abilities to the next level.

When I started my business in 1997, I must have joined just

about every professional women's group and business association in my city because I didn't have a lot of contacts in the corporate world. Although it was uncomfortable at first, I began to slowly meet a lot of wonderful people who generously referred business to me whenever I attended meetings and spoke to civic groups in my community. Over time, my business started to grow as my list of contacts increased.

Although I have trimmed back on some of my professional affiliations, I am still quite active in a handful of organizations and I speak approximately sixty-five times a year to groups throughout the United States. I have learned that we are our best form of advertising for our company every time we get out of our comfort zone and network with other professionals.

Mitzi Perdue, founder of the nonprofit organization Healthy U of Delmarva in Salisbury, Maryland, and daughter of Ernest Henderson, founder of Sheraton hotels, says that volunteering, networking, and being nice to people have opened many doors for her. "Put yourself in a lot of places and you increase your chances of being in the right place at the right time," says Perdue. "It's the law of large numbers. If you're constantly out there, you have a better chance of meeting the right people."

GET A GRIP: GIVE A FIRM HANDSHAKE

A handshake is often the first connection you make with a person, and in the American culture, a good handshake carries a lot of weight. In his book *Panati's Extraordinary Origins of Everyday Things,* Charles Panati discusses the origins of the handshake. According to folklore, handshaking used to be a sign of goodwill. Panati writes, "An ancient villager who chanced to meet a man he didn't recognize reacted automatically by reaching for his dagger. The stranger did likewise and the two spent time cautiously circling each other. If both became satisfied that the situation called for a discussion instead of a fight to the death, daggers were reinserted into their sheaths, and right hands (the weapon hands) were extended as a token of goodwill."

Today, handshaking is still a sign of goodwill and mutual respect. The type of handshake you extend speaks volumes about you and your intentions. A recruiter for a large real estate firm once told me he refuses to hire job candidates who don't stand to shake his hand. Whenever he greets a new applicant, the recruiter makes eye contact, smiles, extends his hand, and introduces himself. "When someone sits there and doesn't stand to shake my hand, I interpret that as a signal that they really don't want to be here," he says. "I consider it a lack of respect and wonder why they are wasting their time and mine."

A handshake is most commonly used to greet someone, bid them farewell, or cement an agreement. It should be warm, friendly, and sincere. A handshake that is too firm or too weak can create a negative impression. Americans seem to prefer handshakes that are on the firm side rather than soft, but there are a few exceptions to the firm handshake. For example, when shaking hands with an elderly person (who might suffer from arthritis, as some do), allow him or her initiate the strength of the grip. Or, if a person's right hand is noticeably impaired in some way, wait to see which hand is offered. When in doubt, let the other person lead the way.

five tips for the perfect handshake

1. All introductions, regardless of the participants' gender, should be accompanied with a firm handshake. Although a man may mean well, some women feel it is condescending when a man shakes her hand delicately and gently or grasps only the tips of her fingers rather than connecting palm to palm.

2. Stand and shake. Standing is more powerful than staying seated, and it shows respect for yourself and for the person receiving the handshake.

3. A handshake should be short and sweet and accompanied with a smile and good eye contact. Some people become slightly uneasy when a handshake lingers for more than a few seconds.

4. In a business setting, a man or a woman can initiate a handshake. In a social setting, it is still acceptable for a man to wait for a woman to initiate a handshake.

5. To show your sincerity when meeting another person, shake hands, then pause briefly before releasing your hand.

WINNING THE NAME GAME

The secret of a good memory is attention, and attention to a subject depends on our interest in it. We rarely forget that which has made a deep impression on our minds.

—TRYON EDWARDS, *theologian*

Most people think it is difficult—if not impossible—to remember names. But guess what? If you think you're bad at remembering names, you will be. Henry Ford once said, "Whether you think you can or whether you think you can't, you're right." Improving your memory skills takes a little bit of work but not as much as you might think.

Remembering names is an essential skill for succeeding in business. It's most likely because when people hear their name, it makes them feel closer and more connected to the person uttering it. Jack Mitchell, CEO of Mitchells/Richards—two upscale clothing stores in Connecticut—and author of *Hug Your Customers: The Proven Way to Personalize Sales and Achieve Astounding Results,* has a simple but winning approach to remembering names. Mitchell's business philosophy is based on personal touches he likes to call "hugs." He believes that what makes people smile and feel good is the little details, like remembering a client's name. To score extra points, Mitchell advises, write down and memorize the names of a person's children, pets, and spouse, as well as the person's hobbies, birthdays, and other significant events. "Remembering someone's name or something about them sends a powerful, warm, fuzzy message that that person is important and valued," says Mitchell.

Dale Carnegie once said, "A person's name is to him or her the sweetest and most important sound in any language." Aren't you flattered and impressed when someone (especially someone of importance) remembers your name? Martha Rogers, Ph.D., a founding partner of the Peppers & Rogers Group, a management consulting firm in Norwalk, Connecticut, remembers when she and three colleagues met Carol Burnett while having dinner in New Orleans. "After Ms. Burnett was introduced to our group, she sat with us for an hour as we laughed and chatted. When Ms. Burnett got up to say good-bye, she called each of us by name. I was blown away and touched by her ability to remember not one, but all of our names after being with us for only one hour," says Rogers.

top ten strategies for remembering names

If you wish to improve your ability to remember names, you must first start with the desire and then be patient and willing to practice every day. These ten strategies will help you perfect this vital business skill:

1. Sharpen your memory with repetition, repetition, repetition. Whenever we do something often enough, it becomes automatic. When you are introduced to someone, say the person's name immediately. For example, say, "It's nice to meet you, Lynn." Repeat the name a few times in conversation or ask the person a question: "Tell me how you know the hosts of this event, Jim." Always conclude the conversation by saying the person's name.

2. Associate a person's name with a character or a movie star. For example, if I met a person named Brad, I would think of the actor Brad Pitt. If I met a woman named Betty, I might think of the character Betty Rubble of *The Flintstones,* or of Betty Boop. The more unusual or bizarre the association, the greater the chance you will remember the person's name.

3. Turn names into visual images and watch the images develop like Polaroid pictures in your mind's eye. For example, if you meet a Tom or Theresa Gardener, imagine this person wearing gardening gloves and planting flowers under a tree.

4. Seeing a name in print makes it easy to remember. When someone gives you a business card, look at the name and say it silently to yourself to make it stick. If the person is wearing a name tag, study their name and face for a few seconds. Whenever you write a person's name down in your day planner, on a note card, or on any other

piece of paper, you program the name in your memory bank and are more apt to recall it later on.

5. If a person doesn't say his name clearly the first time, ask him to repeat it. If the name is difficult to understand or pronounce, ask him to spell it. A person is flattered if you make an effort to say his name rather than not say it at all or calling him something else. My executive assistant Sasheika, whose name can be difficult to pronounce for some, was appalled when a high-ranking executive at a charity luncheon said to her, "I can't remember your name, so can I just call you 'Hey you'?"

6. Don't be embarrassed if you forget names from time to time, even if you just met the person five minutes earlier. Simply say, "It's been a very hectic day—please tell me your name again."

7. If you can't recall someone's name, extend your hand and say your name. The other person will most likely extend her hand and say her name in return.

8. If you can't remember someone's name but can recall where you met him, mention that information. It's better to remember something about a person rather than nothing at all.

9. Associate a person's name with someone you know who has the same name. For example, I recently met a woman named Paige at a chamber of commerce meeting. Her name was easy to remember because it reminded me of my childhood friend named Paige.

10. Don't try to remember too many names at once. Start with one or two at a time, then slowly increase your repertoire each day or with each event you attend.

Any person who is good at remembering names will more than likely admit that it's a skill that must be practiced before it can be perfected. A good memory will enhance your business success. When you remember names, you not only sharpen your memory skills, you make others feel important.

six things to know before you network

Regardless of your profession or whether you have a product or service to sell, you are always selling yourself or your company at large. If you keep an open mind, everyone you meet, personally and professionally, has the potential to help you or tell others about you. The following are six tips to know before you meet and greet:

1. *Make friends first.* Most people buy from, recommend, or hire people they like; therefore networking should be done with the intent to make friends. In time, friendships often blossom into business opportunities.

2. *Think of it as farming, not hunting.* Those who are skilled in networking know the importance of making a genuine connection without being pushy, aggressive, or ostentatious. The goal of networking is to cultivate relationships and gain a person's trust. This does not happen overnight. To see results, constant contact on your part needs to take place.

3. *It's not about you, it's about them.* Dale Carnegie once said, "You can make more friends in two months by becoming more interested in other people than you can in two years by trying to get other people interested in you." Approach networking with the intent to serve, not to sell. Sam Horn, author of *Tongue Fu!: How to Deflect, Disarm, and Defuse Any Verbal Conflict* and perennial emcee of the Maui Writers Conference, recommends curiosity over calculation.

Horn defines "calculation" as the act of sizing up someone in terms of what they can do for you. Will they give you any business? Will they recommend you? Might they hire you? Horn says when you have curiosity, you have a genuine interest in finding out about others and how you might be able to add value for them.

4. *Help others and you help yourself.* True networking is about helping others for mutual gain or satisfaction. If you hear someone say they are looking for a dentist, you could say, "I know a great dentist and I will e-mail her phone number to you." You create or strengthen a relationship when you do a favor for someone. As the saying goes, what goes around comes around. People remember acts of kindness and when they or one of their friends need you or your products or services, thanks to your generosity, they will be more apt to remember and recommend you.

5. *Planning precludes poor performance.* Like a sailing excursion, networking is more effective if you chart your course before the trip. Do some research ahead of time and keep an agenda in mind. Know why you're attending the meeting or event and keep in mind whom you hope to meet or see again. If you know a particular person will be present and you want to meet him, find out as much as possible about this individual. Find out if you have anything, such as hobbies, in common. If you do, it will be much easier to start a conversation and establish a connection. Before networking with someone from outside your company, look at their corporate Web site, if they have one, for recent press releases, news articles, and a biography. Jot down interesting information on index cards and review the cards just prior to the event so the information is fresh in your memory.

6. *Everyone you meet is a potential contact.* No matter where you are, everyone you encounter has the potential to make a difference in your life. You must first be willing to embrace new people and the

ideas, suggestions or opportunities they present to you. When Keith Ferrazzi, CEO of Ferrazzi Greenlight, a consulting and training and development firm in Los Angeles, and author of *Never Eat Alone: And Other Secrets to Success, One Relationship at a Time,* hears or reads about interesting people, he enters their names into his computer. He maintains call sheets by region, listing the people he knows and those he'd like to know, and when he's in town he phones. There are thousands of contacts on Ferrazzi's list, and some of them he hasn't met yet. He calls those "aspirational" contacts. Ferrazzi says, "Build your network before you need it. When someone comes to me for advice on how to build a network because they need a job now, I tell them it's useless. People can tell the difference between desperate attempts to connect and an earnest effort to create a relationship."

seven networking pitfalls

The fastest, most cost-effective way to build your sphere of personal and professional contacts is through word-of-mouth referrals. People who know and like you will refer you, your company, or your products or services to others. After all, people feel more comfortable doing business with those they know, like, and trust rather than giving business to a stranger. There was a time when people said, "It's not what you know, it's who you know." Today's version is, "It's not what you know or who you know, it's who knows you." The following will alert you to some networking pitfalls:

1. ***Don't let your stomach be your guide.*** If your first instinct at a business or social gathering is to make a beeline for the food as soon as you walk into the room, don't be so hasty. To curb the hunger

pangs, eat a substantial lunch or a protein-rich snack before party time so you don't fall prey to the common comfort zones—the bar and the buffet. If hors d'oeuvres or canapés are passed, be selective about what foods you choose to eat. Generally, foods that can be eaten in one bite are less messy. Small foods can also be swallowed much faster in the event someone asks you a question. Large hors d'oeuvres are more difficult to manage and may crumble onto your dress or suit or get all over your fingers.

2. ***Don't juggle your food and drink.*** Handshaking is impossible when you have a drink in one hand and a plate full of food in the other. Mingle first, eat later. If you hold your drink in your left hand at all times, this will allow you to keep your right hand free in case someone wants to shake your hand.

3. ***Loose lips sink ships.*** Just because the drinks are free—and even when they aren't—don't overindulge. Either pass on the alcohol or limit yourself to one or two drinks whenever you're representing your company inside or outside the organization. Eric Strauss, business consultant for IBM Global Services in Fairfax, Virginia, told me he saw a friend ruin his reputation by drinking too much at a party. "My friend, who is a financial advisor, was so intoxicated, I thought to myself, 'I can't imagine anyone wanting to discuss their finances with him.' From that point forward, I never quite thought of him the same way again," says Strauss.

4. ***Don't be a wallflower.*** When you represent your company at any event, don't socialize only with people you know or work with. Introduce yourself to a group of fresh faces who look approachable or someone who is sitting alone. When you and a colleague attend an event together, sit at separate tables. This increases your chances of meeting a lot of fascinating people who might turn into friends or customers.

When Steve Watts, CEO of Bold Approach, a sales, marketing, and public relations consulting firm in Boise, Idaho, sits down at a table with a group of strangers, he usually makes a point of initiating introductions by asking, "Has everyone met each other yet?" If people in the group say no, he will begin by introducing himself. He believes doing this helps to gain credibility because you are doing something nobody else wants to do or has the courage to initiate.

5. *Avoid unwelcome and unsavory topics and office gossip.* Common sense tells us that bringing up personal matters, such as sex, politics, religion, health problems, money problems, or telling tasteless jokes makes others feel uncomfortable. Mean-spirited gossip is unprofessional and hurtful, and it shows a lack of consideration for other people's feelings. You reveal much about your own character when you talk about others behind their backs. Your listeners will wonder, if you're inclined to speak unfavorably about others, what will stop you from speaking that way about them. If you encounter someone who engages in office gossip or talks about a topic that causes you some discomfort, you can excuse yourself from the conversation, mention that you're not comfortable talking about that subject, or turn to the nearest person and change the subject.

6. *Don't leave home without your business cards.* Business cards are called business cards for a reason—they generate business. Your card reflects on you and your business and should be simple, professional, and easy to read. You should carry a supply of cards with you at all times because you never know when a casual encounter might turn into a business opportunity. In most cases, it's best to wait for someone to request your card before giving it out, because if you offer your card too early in the conversation, you may appear too forward or pushy. When someone asks for your card, present it with the

written material facing their direction. When you receive someone's card, look at it for a few seconds, as a sign of respect, before putting it away. As soon as possible, jot down some notes about the person on the back of her card so you can remember where you met her and what you talked about. It's best to avoid doing this in the person's presence. Also, be aware that in many cultures people take pride in their business card, and writing on or defacing it is a faux pas. If you're in a meeting and you've just exchanged business cards with others in the room, place the cards on the table in front of you so you can remember names and distinguish who is speaking.

7. **Respect a person's time.** The best way to conclude a conversation is to end it gracefully, shake hands, and show your gratitude. Say something like, "I've enjoyed speaking with you but don't want to take up too much of your time. I look forward to seeing you again." Perhaps you may want to make an appointment to continue your conversation at a more convenient time. This will give you another opportunity to make a connection.

three tips for feeling included, not excluded

We've all experienced times where we've attended parties and other events and didn't know a single person in the room. Our nerves take over and anxiety immediately sets in. Here are some ways to overcome the misery of mingling with a roomful of strangers:

1. **Pretend you're the host.** If you stand several feet away from the door and greet others as they walk into the room you will start to feel like the host. In addition, you will always have someone to talk to. During the course of the evening, move around the room and

introduce yourself to other guests. Always state your first and last name and, if you're at a business function, include the name of the company you represent. Mitzi Perdue shared with me her definition of a guest and a host. "The guests are those who wait for someone to help them feel comfortable. Hosts are those who take it upon themselves to go out there and try to make other people feel comfortable. It's a lot more fun being a host, because you're in control. You can go around making other people feel great," says Perdue.

2. *Ask a "connector" for help.* If you're uncomfortable introducing yourself to strangers, look for a connector. This person can be extremely helpful when you are a first-timer at an event and you're a bit nervous but still want to meet people. In some cases, this is a person who helped plan and implement the event. For example, the connector may be a board member, a special-event planner, a director of marketing, or the person responsible for announcements or introductions. Find a connector, then introduce yourself and say, "I'm new to this association and I was wondering if you would introduce me to some of the other members." Most people will appreciate your honesty and gladly introduce you to others in the room. If there is someone specific you'd like to meet, such as a CEO, a high-profile person, or an honored guest, seek out a connector to introduce you. You'll be less nervous or intimidated to meet someone if you're formally introduced to them.

There may come a time when you are asked to be a connector for your company, club, or association. Colette Robicheau, a marketing consultant in Halifax, Nova Scotia, is frequently a connector for her clients. She likes to make her clients look good and introduce them to as many influential contacts as possible whenever she accompanies them to events. First, she scopes out the room and chooses three to five potential business contacts to introduce to her client. Then she briefs her client before introducing him. "By introducing my client to an influential guest at the party it turns a cold call into a warm call and creates a firmer foundation on which the two may start a business relationship," says Robicheau.

When introducing others, always introduce the less important person to the more important person, regardless of gender. In business, the order in which an introduction is made is determined by accomplishments and seniority. For example, you would say, "Mr. More Important, I'd like to introduce to you Mr. Less Important." If you're ever given the job of making introductions, learn how to pronounce each person's name, then find out the person's title, and who outranks whom. You'll be surprised how confident you'll feel if you know how to make a proper introduction.

3. *Volunteer to help.* Go from being an outsider to being an insider by volunteering to help. Introduce yourself to someone who has a leadership role in the event. Tell them you are a newcomer and would like to help with registration, setting up, greeting guests, or anything else that needs to get done. When you volunteer, it gives you a feeling of actually belonging instead of merely wanting to belong.

GIVE RELATIONSHIPS TIME TO GROW

As the Supremes once sang, "You can't hurry love / No, you just have to wait." Like personal relationships, business relationships need time to grow and flourish. Friendships and business relationships cannot be rushed. A rapport must first be established before a person will do business with you or recommend you, your product, or your service to others. Relationships thrive on commitment, graciousness, and patience.

No one becomes an "overnight success" overnight. Go to as

many events as you can and eventually you will see your sphere of contacts expand. Networking involves planting seeds in many different places over a period of time. Eventually, when you least expect it, the seeds of your efforts will sprout into relationships and your credibility, and perhaps your popularity, will flourish.

STAYING IN TOUCH

> One of the greatest victories you can gain over someone is to beat him at politeness.
>
> —JOSH BILLINGS, *American humorist*

There's more to networking than mingling with existing clients and potential clients. Most of your networking can take place within your own company, profession, or industry. But regardless of where you network and with whom, it should never end with a handshake. The secret to networking success is staying in touch with every interesting person you meet. Follow-up is paramount if you want to foster long-lasting relationships with new friends, colleagues, clients, and customers. The following are some ways to stay connected long after you say good-bye to someone.

Call or send an e-mail. After meeting someone new, record their name and contact information into your Rolodex, professional address book, or onto your computer, or PDA (personal data assistant). Contact-management software, like ACT!, File-Maker, Microsoft Outlook, or GoldMine, can help you easily manage this information and can be found at most office supply stores or on the Internet. Mark your calendar or create a tickler file as a reminder to reconnect with clients, colleagues, or customers on a monthly, quarterly, or annual basis. A telephone call or an e-mail message is the fastest way to say hello, but brief handwritten notes or holiday cards are more personal and create a lasting impression. There's no need to write a lengthy note. The most effective messages are short and to the point. For example, you might write, "Just a note to say I was thinking of you today and hope your business is going well. Let's stay in touch and get together for a cup of coffee the next time you're in town."

Harvey Mackay, author of *Swim with the Sharks without Being Eaten Alive,* believes that a Rolodex is the cornerstone of success for many people. "From the time I was eighteen years old, my father taught me to put every person I meet in the Rolodex file," says Mackay. "He told me to write a little bit about each person on the back of their card and then find a creative way to keep in touch." That's what Mackay has been doing all his life. He has gone from zero to fifteen thousand names, which are now kept on his computer.

Send magazine or newspaper clippings. Clipping articles is a small gesture that makes a big impact. Whenever Coleman Finkel, president of the Coleman Center in New York City, reads an article that might benefit, entertain, or interest someone he knows, he sends it along with a short handwritten note. "Writing notes is a personal touch, and even though my handwriting isn't the best, people excuse it because those two or three lines are so personal. It's the gesture that's important," says Finkel.

If you read newspapers and periodicals on the Internet, keep your eyes open for articles that will appeal to those you wish to stay in contact with. When you find an article that will interest someone you know, send him an e-mail containing a link to the article. Your note could read, "Tim, I found this article and immediately thought of you and the project you're currently working on. Click on the link below to read the entire article. Looking forward to talking to you soon!"

Send a congratulatory note. Whenever you read an article about someone you know who has received an award or promotion, clip the article and send a note saying something like, "Congratulations on your new promotion! I thought you might appreciate an extra copy of your honorable mention. Best wishes for continued success!"

Bob Danzig, former CEO of Hearst Newspaper Group and teacher of a course on confidence at New School University in New York City, made it a point to show his appreciation to clients when he was head of one of the newspaper properties in upstate New York. "Anytime an advertiser or one of their family members' pictures appeared in our paper, I had the photo elegantly framed, then I sent it to them along with a note saying, 'I thought you would like this affirmation that our paper has good news in it today,'" says Danzig.

Send an electronic newsletter. Margie Fisher, president of Margie Fisher Public Relations in Boca Raton, Florida, says she e-mails free publicity tips twice a month to those who subscribe to her electronic newsletter. A print or electronic newsletter is nonintrusive and people can read it whenever they have time. In addition, it establishes immediate credibility when it provides useful information and is an easy way to stay in touch more frequently than a card or phone call. "I have more than twelve hundred subscribers on my e-zine list and there is no way I can contact each and every one on a regular basis except through my newsletter," says Fisher. Recently, Fisher said she was hired by one of her e-zine subscribers who attended one of her PR workshops about a year ago. This piece of business undoubtedly came about as a result of Fisher's frequent contact with this subscriber.

One of the keys to success in business is staying visible and being remembered favorably. As a result of your reaching out and staying in touch, you won't ever be out of sight, out of mind. E-mail, cards, and clippings cost little yet leave priceless impressions.

TIPS FROM THE TOP

Stand whenever you shake someone's hand.

Say a person's name two or three times in conversation.

Ask, "What can I do for others?" not, "What can others do for me?"

Don't be a wallflower and wait for others to approach you.

Stay in touch by sending notes, e-mail, and news clippings.

Chapter 5

SMALL-TALK SAVVY AND
EFFECTIVE LISTENING

Never speak of yourself to others; make them talk
about themselves instead; therein lies the whole art of
pleasing. Everybody knows it, and everyone forgets it.

—EDMOND AND JULES
DE GONCOURT, *French*
literary collaborators

A topic such as the weather may seem trivial or
unimportant, but American humorist Kin Hub-
bard once said, "Don't knock the weather; nine-
tenths of the people couldn't start a conversation if it didn't
change once in a while." Small talk breaks the ice, activates conversation, and opens up the possibility of forming new relationships. Dr. Bernardo J. Carducci, director of the Shyness Research
Institute at Indiana University Southeast and author of *The Pocket
Guide to Making Successful Small Talk: How to Talk to Anyone, Anytime, Anywhere, about Anything,* says every great romance and
every big business deal begins with small talk. "The key to successful small talk is learning how to *connect* with others, not just
talk with them," says Carducci. While some believe that small

talk is an innate talent, it is, in fact, an acquired skill. The more you do it, the better you get.

Ask good questions and then listen. A favorite topic of conversation for most people is themselves. If you ask open-ended questions starting with "Tell me . . ." or "What do you enjoy most about . . . ," rather than questions that will elicit only a yes or no response, you'll find that the conversation will flow more smoothly. You might try selecting a topic of conversation that demonstrates interest in the other person: "I'm planning to take a vacation this summer. Do you have any favorite places you've been that you recommend?" or "What do you enjoy most about attending these meetings?" By asking questions, you are more prone to focus on the other person and less on yourself.

Identify a bond or commonality you share with another person. It can be as simple as asking about a person's hobbies or interests, complimenting someone on an eye-catching accessory, or commenting on cultural or current events or seasonal festivals. Small talk, when done well, puts others at ease, identifies common interests, and links you with another person.

Give a sincere compliment. Small talk may start with a sincere compliment, but be cautious. In general, it's advisable to compliment someone on their business accomplishments or talents versus their physical attributes. But Barbara Corcoran of the Corcoran Group says that nothing works better for her than starting a conversation with a genuine compliment. "I think the only thing you can sincerely compliment a person on as soon as you meet is something physical, because most times, it's all you have to go on. If you can't compliment someone's hair or eyes, then move on to their blazer, tie, or outfit. When someone asks me if I've lived in New York very long, it doesn't make a connection. That kind of question leaves you really having to work the conversation. Most people enjoy compliments because they don't hear enough of them," says Corcoran.

Know a little about a lot of things. The best conversationalists tend to be great storytellers and are well versed in countless subjects. To acquire a well-rounded repertoire of conversational topics, read books, magazines, and trade journals. Listen to talk radio programs, attend classes, go to cultural and sporting events, and watch a variety of movies.

Nancy Brinker, founder of the Susan G. Komen Breast Cancer Foundation and former U.S. Ambassador to Hungary, shared with me her mother's sage advice about being a gracious, well-informed guest. "My mom used to say if you get an invitation to a party and you show up, it's your obligation to be entertaining. If you're not going to be pleasant, don't go," says Brinker. "Read the newspaper, know something about the other guests, and don't talk about yourself. If you're going to accept an invitation, don't sit in a chair like a lump. Come to the party with a few clean jokes and a couple of interesting things to talk about. And most of all, don't be boring."

Whenever Patricia Thorp, president of Thorp & Company, a public relations firm in Coral Gables, Florida, travels out of town for a business trip, she picks up a copy of the local paper and reads it so she can become acquainted with the issues going on in that particular city. "To win and keep a client requires a consultant to quickly establish bonds of rapport and trust. For example, there may be a five-minute wait for a meeting to begin. Spending that time with a member of the client team can either be fraught with silence and uneasy conversation or can be an opportunity to have a lively discussion about local news," says Thorp. When you're well read, small talk becomes less of a challenge and you will be more at ease conversing with coworkers, colleagues, and clients on any level.

Don't exclude spouses and partners. It's not uncommon to talk shop at parties. However, if you focus too much attention on work-related matters, you may unintentionally alienate any spouses and partners who are present. If you are the host and an important client insists on talking shop, excuse yourself from those you're with and escort the client to another part of the room to finish the conversation. Keep your conversation brief and don't leave your guests unattended too long, as you run the risk of annoying them. If a coworker wants to talk shop, it would be polite in most instances to turn to him and say, "Ian, that's an interesting observation and I think we should save it for later when we're back at the office."

six conversation stoppers

Small talk is easy when someone is genuinely interested in what you have to say and when you're interested in what they have to say. But beware: during one of your networking encounters you're bound to meet a conversation stopper. These dialogue destroyers are masters at feeding their own ego, insecurities, or competitiveness. Watch out for the following six personality types you may stumble upon along the way. Also pay close attention to your own communication style so that you don't fall into these behaviors:

1. THE BRAGGART

This person wants to leverage his status by letting you know how much money he makes or the many material things he or members of his family own. He may say, "The insurance on my sixty-foot Hatteras has skyrocketed in the past year—I just can't believe it." Or, "Linda and I got a great deal on a little place in the Hamptons. It cost us just over a mil."

2. THE RUMOR MONGER

This is the office gossip. A busybody, she always tries to make everybody else's business her own. Also known as the "town crier," she feels in control when she's spreading rumors and juicy gossip about other people. "Did you hear that Mary and Joe aren't seeing each other anymore? I hear that he is going back to his wife." Whenever you encounter the Rumor Monger, change the subject or excuse yourself before she monopolizes your time with her tall tales.

3. THE ONE-UPPER

This person wants you to know that wherever you've been or whatever you've done, he was there first. This person has to feel one step above the rest and isn't shy about letting you know about all of his accomplishments. "You just returned from an Alaskan cruise? My wife and I went on that same cruise two years ago but this year we're going all out and taking a cruise around the world!" The One-Upper likes to feel important. Although it may be difficult, be patient and give this person some attention. Listen and ask questions. "That's wonderful about your cruise around the world. Whenever I go on a cruise, I look forward to the delicious food. What do you enjoy most about cruising?"

4. THE HARD-HEARTED

This person often talks out of turn and says whatever is on her mind without any regard for others' feelings. She doesn't think before she speaks, and she often says things that are inappropriate or embarrassing to others. "Is that all you're going to eat? It's no wonder you're so skinny. It wouldn't hurt if you put on a few pounds."

The Hard-Hearted oftentimes doesn't know how to express herself or her concern for others without sounding rude or negative. If you encounter someone like this, try not to get defensive. Dispel a negative comment with a kind or humorous response. "Lynn, I appreciate your concern but I'm saving my appetite for dinner. Besides, I'm trying to lose a few pounds so I can look as good as you."

5. THE PICK-YOUR-BRAINER

This person is a taker, not a giver. Always looking for free advice, he corners you when you least expect it and wants to "pick your brain" by asking endless questions: "You're a heart surgeon? I've been experiencing these chest pains and I wish you could tell me what's going on." One way to handle the Pick-Your-Brainer is to say something like, "My office hours are nine a.m. to five p.m. If you call me on Monday I'll be happy to schedule a consultation."

6. THE RAMBLER

All of us have had the experience of being held hostage at a party by a Rambler. This person tends to monopolize the conversation or talk only about herself. Whenever you encounter this person, your mind may be tempted to shift into conversation termination mode.

In his book, *The Pocket Guide to Making Successful Small Talk: How to Talk to Anyone, Anytime, Anywhere, about Anything*, Bernardo Carducci writes that inept small talkers spend too much time focusing on their favorite topic. According to Carducci, "They think they are being social because they are talking. But they dominate the conversation, talking *at* somebody, not *with* someone."

The Rambler may also display all the traits of a chronic nonlistener—interrupting others or switching topics like a driver who doesn't believe in using turn signals. After meeting someone like this, you go away feeling unimpressed, uninterested, and unimportant.

Fleeing from the Rambler takes some finesse if you want to maintain your reputation or spare her feelings. The following are some options for handling the Rambler.

Introduce the Rambler to someone else. In other words, find a person in the room she may have something in common with and introduce the two of them. You can say, "From what you just told me, it sounds like you have a passion for riding horses. My friend Pat is an equestrian. I'd like to introduce the two of you." Or, you might try saying "I'd like to refresh my drink" and signaling that you're about to move. If the Rambler insists on going with you to the bar, find someone you can introduce him to along the way. After the introduction has been made, excuse yourself and proceed to the bar alone.

Excuse yourself and move to another location. One way to conclude a conversation with a Rambler is to say something like, "It's awfully warm in here. Will you please excuse me? I've got to get some fresh air." One of my clients says whenever she wants to move away from a Rambler, she tells him she needs to go to the restroom. "This instantly puts an end to the conversation since no further explanation is necessary," she says.

Get another person involved in the conversation. If you and another person get trapped by a Rambler, wait until she takes a breath, then turn to the person next to you and say something like, "Lee, I'd certainly like to have your thoughts on this issue." When you bring another person into the conversation, you take the spotlight off the Rambler and give someone else an opportunity to speak.

Larry Johnson, business consultant and coauthor of *Absolute Honesty: Building a Corporate Culture That Values Straight Talk and Rewards Integrity,* recommends using the "I.S.A.C." technique when dealing with the Rambler. His tips will help you keep your sanity intact and allow you to stay in control so you can move on whenever you feel the time is right.

I = interrupt. Listen for a point in the conversation where you can gently interrupt.

S = summarize. Rephrase what the Rambler just said no matter how mundane it is.

A = ask. Ask questions. This may fly in the face of what you would like to do but if you simply tune the Rambler out, she maintains control of the conversational flow. By summarizing and asking questions, you can guide the conversation in another direction.

C = conclude. Stay in control and assertively wrap up the conversation. You might say, "Barb, I'm delighted to have had an opportunity to talk with you, and if you will excuse me now, I just noticed someone I need to speak to. I hope we can continue this conversation at some other point." Or, "Barb, I hope you get your situation resolved soon. I'm sorry I have to cut our conversation short, but I need to take care of another matter. It was great talking with you." Then conclude with a smile and a handshake.

Johnson says the secret to successfully ending a conversation with a Rambler is to *engage* before you *disengage.* In other words, if you want to steer the discussion in your direction, it's essential to listen and participate in the conversation. Then, when you feel the time is right, you can diplomatically close the conversation and move on without fear of being rude or offensive.

EFFECTIVE LISTENING

Be a good listener. Your ears will never get you in trouble.

—FRANK TYGER, *author*

If you're not listening, you're not learning. By listening to clients, customers, and coworkers you can become much better attuned to their needs and assist them accordingly. At the office, being available and listening to your coworkers' issues or simple day-to-day exchanges can open your eyes to situations or successes that you might otherwise may not have been aware of. You won't be able to solve a person's problems if you use a one-size-fits-all approach to every situation. Like a doctor, you first have to listen to others, then ask questions, check for symptoms, diagnose a situation, and prescribe proper treatment. Would you have confidence in an auto mechanic if he didn't listen to the engine, run a series of tests, or listen to you explain the trouble you were having with your car?

In the workplace, we all like to feel that our opinions and suggestions are valued. From time to time, set aside some time to check in with coworkers and solicit their feedback. Letters, telephone calls, and e-mail work well, but nothing is more effective than meeting with someone face to face. Regardless of whether you agree or disagree with what someone has to say, just listen. Employees will be more open and honest if they are encouraged to express their ideas and concerns without the fear of being judged or criticized. Take time to listen to employees on all levels. It's not always the most senior people who have the best ideas; if given the opportunity, junior employees can add new ideas and fresh perspectives to help the company save time and money or be more efficient.

If you get too busy to listen to what your clients or customers want to tell you, you may lose their business. A friend of mine told me how annoyed she was with her real estate agent after spending an entire day looking at homes that didn't appeal to her. "Everything the agent showed me was either too big or out of my price range," she said. "Did you tell her exactly what you were looking for?" I asked. "I told her I wanted a small, one-bedroom, one-bath house located in a quiet neighborhood. Instead of listening to me, she kept showing me these expensive homes with three and four bedrooms!" she exclaimed. "I think I'll just drive around tomorrow and look on my own." The real estate agent killed an entire day and a potential sale pushing a bigger, more expensive house on her client after the client had told her what she wanted.

BEING ATTENTIVE BUILDS TRUST

Practice attentive listening over selective listening. Attentive listening focuses your energy on the words that are being said and what they mean to the person who utters them. Selective listening is when you hear only certain parts of the conversation then interpret what they mean to you. Former Hearst Newspaper Group CEO Bob Danzig told me he believes anyone can develop better attentive listening skills. "Like anything else, we first have to decide that what's being said is important and then make it a priority," says Danzig. In his Confidence Course at New School University, Danzig teaches his students how to have more successful conversations. He says attentive listening involves looking someone in the eye, using their name in conversation, and responding in such a way that they know you are really listening to them.

"We've all encountered situations where we get into conversations with someone but we aren't sure they're listening," says Danzig. "Their eyes wander or they ask you a question and you start to answer, then they interrupt or they appear to be looking over your shoulder."

Situations like this are awkward because you don't know whether to continue talking or stop and walk away. You feel diminished. To capture the attention of someone who is looking around the room and not focusing on you, try using their name in conversation or moving a little closer to them while asking a question. If they still seem distracted, you could say something like, "Ted, you seem to be a little preoccupied at the moment. May I contact you tomorrow to go over the details of this project?" If the person is an important contact for you, you might want to wrap up the conversation, then approach him a little later or make an appointment with him to talk in private. Just walking away without any type of closure could make you appear uninterested or rude and could hurt your chances of connecting with this person again in the future.

ten ways to become a better listener

1. *Ask pertinent questions.* Questions are the hallmark of a good listener. Asking questions demonstrates a sincere interest in the other person. When you want to understand what a person is trying to say, use clarifying questions such as, "If I hear you correctly, you are saying . . . Is that right?" If you don't understand a person's statement and need more information, ask for specifics. For example, if someone says, "My manager can be so rude and insensitive whenever he

talks to his administrative assistant on the phone," you could ask for specifics by saying, "Give me an example or two of some of the rude things he says so I can better understand what you mean."

2. ***Practice empathic listening.*** The highest form of listening involves empathy. Empathic listening is when you strive to understand how the speaker feels. You don't have to agree with the speaker or even sympathize, but you can better identify with what is being said by using your emotions and intellect. In other words, you listen not only with your ears but with your eyes and heart.

In his book *The 7 Habits of Highly Effective People,* best-selling author Stephen Covey writes, "Most people do not listen with the intent to understand; they listen with the intent to reply." Whenever you begin to craft a response before someone has finished their thought or argument, then you are not fully listening and taking in all the speaker's words and the meaning behind them. Covey emphasizes the importance, the power, and the necessity of not merely going through the motions of ordinary listening but opening oneself to the talker in an attempt to feel what that person is feeling. Covey believes that the only way to establish communication in some professional and personal situations is by standing for a moment in another's shoes and seeing the world through that person's eyes. Put yourself in the person's situation and ask, "How would I feel if this were happening to me?" This is something we are all capable of, but few of us rarely—if ever—deliberately go to this level when we listen.

For example, one of my students, who had recently moved to the United States from India, told me how difficult it was for him to read a menu whenever he went to a fancy restaurant. He told me about the time he went on a job interview over lunch and didn't know what many of the items on the menu were. As I listened to him, I imagined how I felt many years ago when my date took me to an upscale French restaurant for dinner. I couldn't pronounce many items on the menu since I wasn't familiar with French cuisine, therefore I didn't know what to order. Immediately, I could feel his pain as I began to relate to his anxiety and frustration.

3. ***Listen with your entire body.*** Nodding occasionally, making eye contact, taking notes, and being fully engaged all demonstrate genuine concern for the person you are speaking with. Watch the speaker's facial expressions, hand gestures, and eye contact. Allow the speaker to finish her sentence before you interject your thoughts or opinions, because you will likely dilute or detract from the speaker's message.

4. ***Share personal stories.*** Asking someone to share stories often creates a firm, personal connection that can enhance the business connection. Most people enjoy "telling their story," so when I go to dinner parties I often ask couples, "So, how did you meet each other?" In many cases this question encourages scintillating conversation and gives me the opportunity to learn more about a person. When you share personal stories about yourself in which others can relate, you immediately break down any barriers between you and the listener and you are perceived as more approachable and down-to-earth. Perhaps that's why our society is so fascinated by watching reality television shows that feature celebrities. We want to know that they're real people too.

5. ***Paint a visual picture.*** Don't simply listen to what a person is saying, create a visual image of what is being said. This will help you follow and understand a story and remember it later on. Your clients and colleagues will be impressed that you hung on to every word and made them feel like the most important person in the room.

6. ***Don't interrupt.*** Many bright, talented executives interrupt or finish other people's sentences without realizing it. A bank vice presi-

dent once told me his reason for finishing sentences was this: "If I finish my customers' sentences, they'll know I understand what they are talking about." What he doesn't realize is that jumping in does a disservice to his customers and prevents them from completely expressing their feelings or opinions. Except in the case of an emergency, interrupting others will make them think you're in a hurry or trying to put words into their mouth.

Paul Donahue, executive vice president and CFO (chief financial officer) of Wackenhut Services Incorporated, a leading paramilitary and security company, admits to being guilty at times of "overtalking." "In the past," he says, "I have anticipated what others might say because I viewed this as a way of showing them that I was prepared or on top of the situation. I called it 'filling in the blanks.' Now when I feel the urge to respond, I wait an extra three seconds and allow the other person to finish his sentence."

7. *Pause before you reply.* Silence, the white space of conversation, has a commanding impact. This powerful communication technique makes people wonder what you're going to say next. Pausing allows you to think about what you're going to say before you say it, and it creates a bit of anticipation for the listener. Pause briefly before giving an answer if you want to create a little suspense or capture your listener's attention.

8. *Eliminate distractions.* If you are speaking to someone who seems distracted, say, "Perhaps this isn't the best time to talk about this. Are you free another time?" On the other hand, if you're the one who's distracted or too busy to talk to someone, let the other person know you're preoccupied at the moment and would rather talk when you're able to give him your undivided attention. If you try to talk to someone about an important topic when you're not ready to listen or while you're performing other tasks, you may unintentionally make

him feel unimportant or frustrated and this could negatively affect your relationship.

When I asked Congressman Mark Foley who he thought was the best listener he ever met, he said Jack Valenti, former president of the Motion Picture Association of America. "I was impressed with Jack the first time I met him in 1995 at the Hay-Adams Hotel in Washington, D.C., while I was a freshman in Congress. Jack was impeccably dressed and he radiated professionalism," Foley recalls. "His vocabulary was lyrical and lush—a testament to what one can do with the English language. He was educated and well-versed, had a calm demeanor, and was focused intently on our conversation. During our one-hour meeting, he never looked around at the others in the room. Although he was very important, he was helpful, gracious, and didn't carry an air of superiority. He earned my respect and admiration immediately and we are still great friends today."

9. *Speak with a purpose.* Our bodies are conveniently designed to listen twice as much as we speak, since we have two ears and only one mouth. Have you noticed that some of the most brilliant people in the world speak only when they have something important or profound to say? When these people talk, we listen, and we hang on their every word. It's oftentimes what we don't say that makes a greater impression on others rather than what we do say.

10. *Don't give unsolicited advice.* If you are an idea generator or a great problem solver, you may be tempted to give a client, friend, or colleague your unsolicited advice without fully listening to the message they want you to hear. While some people may appreciate your "words of wisdom," others may become defensive and think you are trying to change them. One day a colleague shared with me some of her career frustrations. After hearing just a few sentences, I began to give her my advice. Later I learned she got angry because I missed

what was most important. She wanted me to be a sounding board and to listen without giving my opinions. Sometimes it's better to give advice only when you're being paid for it.

Listening effectively is the most fundamental yet powerful communication tool one can possess. But like any skill, it takes time and practice to develop. When you stop talking and truly listen to what others are saying, you overcome communication barriers, and your personal and professional interactions begin to flourish.

TIPS FROM THE TOP

Ask open-ended questions and don't talk about yourself too much.

Find something in common with those you meet.

Pay sincere compliments often.

Listen with the intent to learn.

Don't give someone advice unless he pays for it first.

Chapter 6

DINING FOR DOLLARS:
THE ART OF THE MEAL

It isn't so much what's on the table that matters as what's on the chairs.

—W. S. GILBERT, *English playwright and librettist*

According to a survey developed in November 2000 by Robert Half International and conducted by an independent research firm, 49 percent of chief financial officers said their most successful business meetings, outside the office, were conducted at a restaurant. Today, companies place such great importance on making a good first impression over a meal that they go to great lengths to hire job candidates who know the difference between a soup bowl and a finger bowl. It's not at all uncommon for companies to host dinners and receptions for job candidates in order to evaluate their social skills and table manners.

Anymore, being great at your job requires that you get out from behind your desk and break bread with clients and colleagues. To succeed in business, your skills at the dining table must be on par with your skills at the boardroom table. First and foremost, there is no excuse for bad manners. Bread dunking, soup slurping, finger licking, and teeth picking are career-inhibiting behaviors that prompt CEOs to call for an etiquette seminar. Several years ago I got a call from the CEO of a prominent life insurance company who was aghast when he witnessed his vice president of finance dunking his roll in his soup during an important board of directors dinner. This CEO realized that business opportunities could quickly disappear if he allowed his management team to concentrate more on the meal than on a colleague or client. I wound up working with this company for several years until all the managers completed my seminar.

food for thought: how to avoid the fifteen most common dining mistakes

1. Bread should not be eaten as a whole slice or even two halves. You'll look more polished if you break off one bite-size piece, butter it, and then eat it. And don't butter your bread directly from the butter dish. Instead, transfer some butter from the butter dish to your bread plate. Although it can be tempting at times, bread should never be dunked in your soup or used to sop up the juices on your plate.

2. At business meals, it is not necessary for a man to pull out a woman's chair or stand when a woman approaches or leaves the table during a meal. (The only exception to this rule would be if your company's CEO insists upon these courtesies.) If you are a woman and a man holds your chair or opens the door for you, acknowledge the gesture with a kind "Thank you." Today, whoever reaches the door first, regardless of gender, should open it for the other person.

3. If you drop a piece of silverware on the floor while having dinner in a restaurant, leave it and ask the server for another. If you drop your fork while having dinner in someone's home, pick it up and ask the host for another.

4. Pass the salt and pepper shakers together, even if someone asks you to pass one or the other. It's best to keep them together as a set in the event someone else at the table wants both. Don't pass them from hand to hand, as this is considered bad luck in some cultures. Place them in front of the receiver and allow him to pick them up.

5. Don't pick your teeth at the table with your finger, toothpick, knife blade, or sugar packet. If you think you have something stuck between your teeth, go to the restroom and take care of the situation.

6. Don't apply lipstick, or touch your hair at the table.

7. Don't put your handbag, keys, notebook, or cell phone on the table. If your handbag is small, put it on your lap underneath your napkin. Large handbags and briefcases should be placed on the floor next to, or between, your feet. It's best to avoid putting your handbag on the back of your chair because a server might accidentally knock it off or it could get stolen. And remember to set your cell phone on silent or vibrate mode.

8. After using a sugar or sweetener packet, fold the paper and place it underneath your saucer or bread plate.

9. It's not necessary to thank a server each time you are served. Your gratitude can be conveyed with a smile, an occasional thank-you, and a generous tip.

10. If you bite into a bone, a piece of gristle, or something else that you'd rather not swallow, discreetly remove it with your thumb and index finger and place it on the edge of your plate. If you must place the object in your napkin, ask the server for a new napkin as soon as possible.

11. Don't double-dip. That is, don't dip your chip in the salsa, take a bite, then dip the same chip again.

12. Do not push your plate away or stack your dishes after you have finished eating. This will make you appear impatient for your plates to be removed.

13. Wait until everyone at your table has been served before you begin eating. When you are seated with a very large group, you may start eating after four or five people next to you have been served.

14. Don't tuck you napkin into your collar or use it as a handkerchief. Place it on your lap after the host removes his napkin from the table. If you temporarily leave the table to go to the restroom or make a phone call, place your napkin on your chair. This will let the server know you will be returning. When you have finished eating, place your napkin neatly to the left of your plate. If your plate has been removed, place your napkin where your plate was located.

15. When passing food, offer some to your neighbor first before serving yourself, and then pass the food counterclockwise.

First Courses: An Introductory Meeting

Getting acquainted with a client or colleague over a meal is a lot like a first date. You never get a second chance to make a first impression. If you have atrocious manners, you might get passed up for potential business opportunities, regardless of how much talent, experience, or intellect you possess. William Mahoney of Mahoney & Associates says manners and etiquette are a critical part of his company's culture. He says if someone displays poor table manners, he doesn't want to be around them. That's why he has written a business etiquette manual for his employees. Designed to help his staff interact with others in a professional business manner, this comprehensive manual covers topics such as enhancing office relationships, business dress, social etiquette, dining etiquette, and communication skills. "I believe prospective clients vote with their feet and we need not give them any reasons to NOT do business with us. Bad manners, offensive dressing, or inappropriate language will get you either fired or not hired" says Mahoney. "You'll probably never really know why, but the client or prospective employer will."

In *How to Become a Rainmaker,* Jeffrey Fox writes, "If you hold your fork like a gardener's trowel, shovel food into your mouth, make noisy slurping, smacking sounds, or chew and talk simultaneously, you will not get or keep customers. Bad table manners are a sign of a narrow or undisciplined or over-indulged upbringing." Fox goes on to write, "Bad table manners are off-putting; they signal insensitivity to others, an overly self-interested person, and an incomplete education."

Because a meal is often part of the interview process, it pays to know how to handle yourself in any dining situation so that you can land the job. Pat Williams, senior vice president of the Orlando Magic, says if you're over seven feet tall, weigh three hundred pounds, and are one of the fifty top basketball players of all time, like Shaquille O'Neal, a dining mistake may be overlooked. "But if you have just finished attending the Wharton School . . . and you're interviewing with a reputable company, don't engage in a food fight or eat off someone else's plate. That doesn't play well in business," says Williams.

Here are eight strategies to help you whip up good business without winding up with egg on your face, whether you're meeting someone for the first time or closing a deal:

1. ***Select a sweet spot.*** If you invite someone to lunch or dinner, it is your responsibility to select the restaurant. Choose a familiar place so you'll know what to expect in terms of noise level, food quality, and service. Select a restaurant that is not out of the way or inconvenient for the other person. Consider your guest's food preferences: it wouldn't be wise to take a vegetarian to a steak house.

2. ***Know the menu.*** If you're entertaining clients, colleagues, or coworkers in an unfamiliar city, call the restaurant ahead of time and ask for a copy of the menu or go online to see if the menu is listed on the restaurant's Web site. When you call, ask about the specials of the day. If you travel extensively, keep a database of popular restaurants you frequent. If you don't have time to call the restaurant ahead of time, arrive early so you can establish rapport with the manager and waitstaff and familiarize yourself with the menu before your guests arrive.

3. ***Choose comfort over cost.*** You may be tempted to take your guest to an expensive restaurant just because you'd like to eat there and your company is footing the bill. However, your guest may not enjoy or have time for a long, lavish, expensive meal. You can get acquainted with people just as easily in casual places. President Lyndon B. Johnson delighted foreign dignitaries with relaxed, Texas-style outdoor barbecues at his ranch, and these events provided opportunities for long-term friendships to develop.

4. ***Pay in advance.*** Confusion or awkwardness can occur when the check is brought to the table and no one claims it, or the client feels obligated because of hesitation on your part. For business meals, the person who does the inviting does the paying, regardless of age, status, or gender. A hospitable host will also take care of all incidentals, including valet charges and the coat check. When Bob Barrett, CEO of InCharge Institute, a financial wellness company in Or-

lando, Florida, invites clients or colleagues to lunch, he makes certain that the check is never brought to the table. "My executive administrator calls the restaurant, speaks directly to the manager, gives him our company credit card number, and requests that the receipt be sent to our office," says Barrett. Barbara Corcoran of the Corcoran Group says she handles the bill just before dessert, thereby eliminating any issue over who pays for the meal. "I excuse myself and go to the ladies' room and then pay the bill on the way," she says. "I hand my credit card to the maitre d' and then he has the check waiting for me to sign when I come out of the ladies' room."

5. **Choose the perfect table.** To ensure that you have your guest's undivided attention, eliminate as many distractions as possible. Request a table in a quiet location, preferably away from heavy traffic flow, the restrooms, cash register, kitchen, entryway, or bar. Give your guest the best view, generally facing the window or onto the restaurant. If you're dining with one person, you'll find it easier to listen and carry on a conversation if the two of you sit diagonally instead of across from each other. When you have several guests, give your most prominent guest the seat of honor, which is located on your right side.

6. **Give the guest the best.** Oftentimes the guest will want to follow the host's lead and order something similar on the menu; however, a guest takes priority and should order first and be served first. The host orders last and is served last. When you're the host and you're on a daily stipend or have a limited budget, preorder the food or ask the restaurant manager to print a special prix fixe menu containing items that you've chosen or that fall into a certain price range. If you want to let your guest know what to order without saying how much money you expect to spend, you can say something like, "The pasta primavera is outstanding" or "I'm going to have the chicken Caesar

salad." Your guest will probably be inclined to order the same thing or something comparable in price. If you say "I highly recommend the filet mignon" or "The chef is famous for his veal chops," then your guest will probably feel comfortable ordering an entrée in a higher price range. If you're the guest and the host doesn't indicate what you can order, it's safer to order something moderately priced rather than ordering the most expensive item on the menu or ordering too many courses. The host should order the same amount of courses as the guest so the guest doesn't eat alone. In other words, if the guest orders an appetizer, the host should also. If the guest declines dessert, so should the host even if that's the moment you've been waiting for. Pace yourself so you don't finish miles ahead of, or behind, the other diners at your table. Contrary to what your mother told you, it's not necessary to clean your plate to the point where you can see your reflection. In business, it's acceptable to leave a small portion uneaten so you don't appear as though you were starving to death.

7. *Eat first, talk business later.* Generally, it's wise to make small talk and share a few stories with your dining partner before talking about business. By doing this, you and your guest have an opportunity to establish some common ground and get to know each other better. If you're not sure when to discuss business, follow the decision maker's lead. If your guest wants to talk shop and sign a multimillion dollar contract during appetizers, then by all means do so. Or if your time together is limited, business may be discussed as soon as you have ordered from the menu. If you and your guest would rather use the dinner appointment solely as a time to get better acquainted, then set up a follow-up meeting to discuss business. Say something like, "I have some ideas on how I can help you with those concerns you mentioned. Would you like to get to-

gether at my office sometime next week or would you prefer to meet in your office?" When you are the guest, keep in mind that some people will invite you to dinner as a way to build trust and get to know you better personally before making a decision to work with you.

8. *Avoid chewable challenges.* Although succulent spareribs and Alaskan king crab legs may top your list of favorite foods, you'll be better off if you avoid these delectable delights during business meals. Steer clear of foods that are slippery, stringy, messy, cumbersome, unpredictable, or difficult to maneuver. Instead, order items on the menu that are easy to eat so you can give your full attention to your client.

Navigating the Table and Wielding Utensils Like a Pro

There is nothing that gives away one's lack of table manners faster than using the wrong utensil for the wrong purpose or presenting oneself poorly at the table. Some of the basics to keep in mind: don't put your elbows on the table; don't slouch; don't slurp, gulp, or burp; say please and thank you; and treat the waitstaff with kindness. The box below outlines the basics of a place setting. Remember, if you're in unfamiliar territory, be observant and let your host be your guide. If she uses a particular fork for the escargot, follow suit.

> - *"Fork" has four letters and "left" has four letters, so it's easy to remember that forks are located on the left side of your plate.*
> - *"Spoon" and "knife" have five letters each and "right" has five letters, so remember that knives and spoons are placed*

*on the right side of the plate. The blade of the knife always
faces toward the plate.*

- *Always start from the outside and work your way inward.
In other words, use the utensils farthest from the plate first,
then use the utensils closer to the plate in sequence.*
- *The fork and spoon placed at the top of the plate are to be
used for dessert. When dessert arrives, move the fork down
to the left side of your plate and move the spoon down to the
right side of your plate, unless the server does it for you.*
- *Your bread plate is always on the left, and your glasses are
always on the right.*
- *The butter spreader is placed on the bread plate in either a
horizontal or a vertical position, with the blade facing
inward.*
- *Spoons for coffee and tea are generally brought out with the
coffee cups and saucers at the end of the meal or with
dessert.*

Have you ever eaten your neighbor's bread by mistake? If so, you know how embarrassing it can be. To prevent this from happening in the future, remember the saying "Left over bread." Liquids, like your water or wine, will be on the right side of your plate and solids, like your roll, will be on the left side of your plate. If someone accidentally eats your roll, you shouldn't call attention to their mishap or eat your other neighbor's roll in rebellion. Instead, forget about the roll (who needs the carbs anyway?), or discreetly ask the server to bring you another one and place it on the side of your main plate.

Here are three more dining dilemmas you may face when you sit down at a table with your clients or colleagues.

1. *Following the American style versus the Continental style.* In the American style, the fork is held in your left hand while you use your knife with your right hand. After cutting (one bite at a time), place the knife on the upper right-hand edge of the plate, with the blade facing inward, and transfer the fork from your left hand to your right; then bring the food to your mouth with the fork tines up. If you're left-handed, you might find it easier to reverse this method and cut with the left hand instead. When taking a break between bites, place your knife, slanting inward, on the upper right-hand edge of your plate, and place your fork in a similar position in the center of your plate. Left-handed diners may reverse this position. When finished eating, left- and right-handed diners should place the utensils side by side on a slant across the center of the plate (at 10:20 o'clock), with the fork tines facing upward and the blade of the knife facing inward.

In the Continental style, the fork is held in your left hand, tines downward, while you use your knife with your right hand. After cutting, use your knife to push food onto the back of the fork, then bring the food to your mouth with the fork tines down. Left-handed diners may reverse this method and cut with the left hand and eat with the right. When you want to take a break between bites, place your utensils in a crisscross position on the lower part of your plate. When you have finished eating, place the utensils side by side on a slant across the center of the plate (at 10:20 o'clock), with the fork tines facing downward and the blade of the knife facing inward. Left-handed and right-handed diners use the same resting and finished positions. Once you use a piece of silverware, place it on your plate not on the clean tablecloth.

By becoming acquainted with both the American and Continental styles of eating, you can easily adapt to any dining situation throughout the world. Either style is appropriate. However, the Continental style is universally accepted, looks more sophisticated, and is extremely efficient. If you're a left-handed diner you may find the Continental style easier because you don't have to switch utensils from one hand to the other. Regardless of whether you use the American or the Continental style of dining, it's best to use that style consistently throughout the meal. More important, the way you place your silverware on your plate, while you're resting between bites or when you're finished, serves as a signal to help the waitstaff determine whether or not to remove your plate.

2. ***Eating foods you dislike.*** There may be times when you're served a dish you dislike or are unfamiliar with. Try it. You may be surprised to find that you like it. If you don't bother to try it, you run the risk of insulting your host. In some foreign countries, a delicacy may be specially prepared for you. Eat what you can, then move the rest around on your plate, pretend to take a few bites, and chat with your tablemates. If you have food allergies, let your host know well in advance so something else can be prepared for you.

3. ***Handling accidents gracefully.*** Accidents will happen, especially if you frequently entertain or are entertained. When things go wrong, stay calm until the crisis is under control. If you spill a drink, ask a server to bring you extra napkins. If a few pieces of lettuce fall off your plate, discreetly put them back. If you make a mess with your crusty French bread, do nothing. It's best to leave the crumbs alone. In most upscale restaurants, the server will "crumb" the table before dessert is served.

In many cases, humor can deflect potential embarrassment or discomfort. Nancy Brinker told me that during one of her first dinners as an ambassador, she learned to make the best of what might have been a disastrous situation. "One night I hosted a dinner for a group of prominent businesspeople and various government officials at the U.S. residence. That evening, the server accidentally dumped food on one of my guests, a picture fell from the wall, and one of the candles blew up all over the table," Brinker said. "I expected the chandelier to fall from the ceiling, but it didn't, thank goodness! I was very embarrassed because I take great pride in my work. Through it all, I just carried on as if nothing had happened. All the guests were great: I think they felt sorry for me. If you don't make a big deal out of things, people are very forgiving."

BREAKFAST: THE NEW POWER MEAL

Business breakfasts have had a renaissance among those who want to conduct business in a casual, relaxed atmosphere. As business meals become more informal and expense accounts are reduced, there are unique, cost-effective places to entertain clients, vendors, and coworkers. Coffeehouses and diners are becoming increasingly popular because they are fast, convenient, and affordable, and no alcohol is served. In the morning, most of us are fresh and alert, while in the evening, we tend to be more tired and ready to go home. One of my clients told me she turned to business breakfasts after things went awry at a dinner she had arranged for her vendors. Instead of choosing a quiet location, she'd chosen a busy local hot spot for wining and dining. The noise at the bar was so loud she and her guests couldn't hear each other talk. The dinner was supposed to begin at seven-thirty, but her group wasn't seated until much later and the main course wasn't presented until eleven-thirty. Everyone had tired of drinking and their only appetizer was a loaf of bread.

Steve Watts of Bold Approach found out that one of his

clients liked coffee and frequented a particular Starbucks in town. "When I took her to her favorite Starbucks she was in her comfort zone. She knew all the employees and even had a favorite table. We had a two-hour meeting and it turned into one of the best meetings I've had in my entire career." Since then, Steve has continued to conduct quite a bit of business at Starbucks.

Dick Glovsky, a rainmaking employment lawyer at Prince, Lobel, Glovsky & Tye and a former U.S. assistant attorney, believes breakfast is the most important meal of the day. "I use breakfasts as much as, if not more than, lunches," says Glovsky. "It's the beginning of the day, before things heat up. You can have a more relaxed conversation when you meet early and you're not as pressed to hurry to the next meeting."

Glovsky's goal during a business meal: to develop his business. But his first meeting with a prospective client doesn't always revolve around a sale. "There are times when I might not say anything about my business at the first meeting," says Glovsky. "If the person doesn't ask, I'm hesitant to say much. I try to show an interest in him or her and wait until they show an interest in me."

With breakfast meetings replacing the time honored business lunch, get your day off to a good start by avoiding these breakfast blunders:

- It is not necessary to turn your cup upside-down if you don't want coffee. Simply say "No, thank you" to your server when coffee is offered.
- Never use your toast to wipe your plate clean. If you want to enjoy the broken egg yolk on your plate, break off a small piece of toast, place it on your plate, and use your fork to dip it in the yolk and eat it.

- If bacon is crisp, you may eat it with your fingers; otherwise, use a knife and fork and cut one piece at a time.
- When eating soft food, such as an omelet, you may use the side of your fork to cut into it, or you may use a knife and fork.
- Avoid striking the sides of your cup with your spoon when stirring your coffee or tea. Do not lick the spoon after stirring.
- If someone asks for the cream, pass the creamer with the handle facing outward so it's easier for the other person to take hold of it.
- Use your napkin, not your tongue, to clean your fingers after eating a messy bagel or a piece of toast with jelly.
- If you are served oatmeal or cereal in a small cup, place your spoon on the plate underneath the cup when you're resting or when you're finished.
- Avoid overloading your plate with food when you go through a breakfast buffet. It's more polite to take smaller portions and make an extra trip than to fill your plate beyond capacity. When you're ready to go back for more, leave your dirty plate on the table for your server to remove and help yourself to a clean plate.
- If you order hot tea and you're given a tea bag, don't repeatedly dunk the tea bag into the cup of hot water or wrap the tea bag string around a spoon to squeeze out the last drops of tea.

POLISH YOUR DINNER PARTY PROTOCOL

Private dinner parties have made their way into the business world as more people are choosing to entertain colleagues, clients, and coworkers in a warmer, more intimate setting. Dinner parties serve several purposes: to see friends and colleagues for sheer pleasure, to entertain those you wouldn't ordinarily invite but want to solidify a relationship with, and to reciprocate with those who have previously invited you to their party.

Dinner parties not only permit people from different levels, backgrounds, and professions to meet on intimate terms, they also serve as a primary, effective method of advancing social and professional objectives. Author Sam Horn believes in hosting events and parties that will facilitate meaningful connections. "It's a way to put ourselves on the map with people—not by selling, but by initiating and facilitating an event that adds value for everyone involved," says Horn. Here are some hints for you to keep in mind to ensure that your dinner party will be memorable.

- *Choose your guests carefully.* The guest list should be made up of those you know, those you would like to know better, and those invited only to please other guests or to add some excitement due to their stellar reputation. Make sure guests are compatible with other guests before placing them next to one another at the dinner table.
- *Separate cliques and couples.* To keep the conversation lively and interesting, separate couples, those who work together, or those who know each other extremely well. Put together those who might have something in common or might strike up some business in the future. If you're a guest, don't take the liberty of switching place cards if you're not satisfied with the person you're sitting next to. You'll be doing yourself a disservice. If you want to sit with a particular person at a party, call the host ahead of time and request to be seated at that person's table.
- *Offer a diverse menu.* Consider your guests' food preferences and possible allergies and dietary restrictions. In order to accommodate individual needs, serve a variety of foods and provide plenty of non-alcoholic beverages for nondrinkers.

THE BEST GUEST

Every host loves a gracious guest. To ensure that you are invited back for another visit, follow these guidelines.

- *Please respond.* If you're fortunate enough to be invited to a coveted business dinner with an A-list of invitees, a company-sponsored party, or a dinner at your boss's home, respond as soon as possible. Invitations should be responded to within a week of receipt or by the date specified on the invitation. If you wait until the last minute to respond, it may appear as if you are waiting for a more attractive offer to come along. All invitations should be responded to regardless of whether or not you plan to attend. If you tell the host or event planner that you will be attending, be sure to follow through, even if you can stay for only a short while. Don't bring a guest or colleague unless you are invited to do so. An extra person could add extra stress if the host is unprepared. If you promise to attend and find out at the last minute you won't be able to, either call your host the next day to apologize or write a note of apology. Don't send someone in your place without clearing it with the host first. An invitation that includes the word "nontransferable" is intended for the recipient only and should not be given to anyone else. You may forfeit your chances of ever being invited to another event if you aren't considerate enough to accept or decline an invitation. "Regrets only" on an invitation means you should call only if you are unable to attend, otherwise the host will assume you're coming.
- *Bring a gift.* To show your appreciation for the invite, bring a small gift for the host. Attach a card to it so the host will know who brought it. Don't assume the host will remember what you brought

especially if she receives a lot of gifts. If you bring flowers, put them in a vase before giving them to the host or send them the day of the event. A bottle of wine makes a nice gift if you know the host will enjoy and appreciate it. Don't expect the host to serve or show your gift at the party. In many cases, the host may have chosen wines to match the menu. In the words of the late esteemed food writer Craig Claiborne, in his *Elements of Etiquette*, "a host is never obligated to serve a gift of food and drink, and a guest is never justified in feeling slighted if his does not appear on the dinner table."

- *Show your appreciation.* Don't forget to say good-bye to the hosts before you leave and thank them for inviting you. If you have to leave early, simply mention that you have another obligation and you must be going. No other excuse is necessary. Write a thank-you note within forty-eight hours, even if you brought a gift or expressed your thanks verbally.

Ordering and Enjoying Wine

Wine is usually the most popular beverage at a formal dinner or holiday party. But ordering and drinking wine can be intimidating, particularly if you don't have a basic knowledge of wine etiquette. I conferred with wine expert Mark Spivak, editor of *Uncorked! Magazine,* to share his advice, which you will find summarized below.

Few people know that smoking with or prior to drinking wine will affect the wine's taste, as will the odor of cigarettes or cigars for nonsmokers. Always request the nonsmoking section in a restaurant unless the majority of your group insists on sitting at the bar, where smoking is oftentimes allowed.

Chewing gum, eating breath mints, or brushing your teeth

just before drinking wine will also alter its taste. Eat something mild, like bread or crackers, before enjoying a glass of wine.

At a restaurant or house party, the host is responsible for selecting and tasting the wine. If you're a host who is not a wine drinker or is unfamiliar with different types of wine, talk to your server, sommelier, or someone on staff who helped put the wine list together. He or she will gladly assist you. If you defer the responsibility of selecting the wine to someone else at your table, they may feel put on the spot if they don't know how much money you're willing to spend.

If you aren't sure what type of wine you want but know how much you're willing to spend, call the server over and point to a price on the right hand side of the wine list (those in your party won't know what you're pointing to) and say, "I'm looking for a red wine similar to this. We usually drink this at home but we'd like to try something different." A savvy server will then recommend a wine in your price range.

If you'd rather select the wine yourself and aren't sure what to order, look at the wine list and see where the bulk of the selections are listed. For example, if the wines on the list range from $20 to $100 and the majority are in the range of $30 to $50 or $40 to $60, those are most likely the wines that have been carefully selected and that sell more frequently.

The old rule of "white wine with fish or chicken and red wine with meat" no longer applies. It is acceptable nowadays to order the wine that you will most enjoy or one that is compatible with the structure and depth or texture of the dish you'll be eating. For example, if you're having chicken in a rich sauce or a reduced sauce made from a red wine, it's appropriate to order a red wine to complement it. If you wish to order wine for the table and everyone in your party is ordering a different meal, you might choose a light red wine, like a Pinot Noir, that would go with a wide range of dishes. Or, to be safe, order a bottle of red and a bottle of white.

When the server brings a bottle of wine to your table, it's common practice to check the label so you can verify that the type of wine and the vintage matches what you ordered. More than one well-meaning host has found out after the fact that he was charged for a $120 bottle of Merlot when he thought he'd ordered a $60 bottle. Next, look at the wine label to see if it has any stains. If so, this may be an indication that something happened in the course of shipping or storage, or the wine may be bad.

If you order two bottles of the same type of wine, it's customary to taste both bottles. Although the first bottle may taste fine, it's wise to check the second bottle to ensure consistency of taste and enjoyment. The time to decide whether a bottle of wine is acceptable or not is when you initially taste it. Once that time has passed, it's too late.

When the server removes the cork there is no need to sniff it. Unless you are a wine expert, there isn't much to tell from examining a cork. Besides, screw caps and synthetic corks are quickly replacing natural corks. Furthermore, many wines are stored standing up and the cork may be dry.

Even if you are not a wine expert, it's essential to smell the wine before serving it to your guests. After your server pours a small amount of wine into your glass, swirl it around and smell the bouquet of fruit, flowers, wood, herbs, or spices: a good, unspoiled wine always has a pleasant aroma. If the wine has a musty odor or smells like damp cardboard, it should be sent back. If the wine meets with your approval, your server will pour wine for all your guests, starting with the guest of honor. Depending on the size of the glass, your server will generally pour either a half or a third of a glass of wine.

Hold both red and white wine glasses by the stem. This keeps your hand from warming the wine and it's easier to swirl the wine in the glass when you hold the stem. Avoid wearing heavy perfume if you plan on drinking wine or offering it to guests; it can interfere with the aroma of a wine.

If you wish to skip the wine, don't turn your glass upside down; simply say "No, thank you" to the server, and your glass will be removed. There is no need to explain that you are allergic to the wine, or that it gives you headaches, or that it immediately goes to your head. Similarly, it's not polite to ask someone why they aren't drinking alcohol. If you find yourself in the company of someone who has obviously had too much to drink, discreetly refrain from pouring more wine in their glass and offer them more food.

TASTEFUL TOASTING

A toast is the perfect way to recognize a special occasion or celebration. The custom of raising the first glass of wine to one's health has been traced to ancient Greece, where a sip was taken to demonstrate that the drink was not poisoned. To ward off evil spirits, guests would clink their glasses together—a tradition that is still practiced today. The tradition of clinking glasses together also dates back to the Borgia family, Spanish aristocrats who were firmly established in Italy when Alfonso Borgia was named Pope (Calixtus III) in 1455. The infamous Lecrezia Borgia was said to have poisoned any number of rivals by dropping lethal fluids into their drinks. The splashing of wine from cup to cup became a safeguard against poisoning.

It is customary for the host to propose a toast at the beginning of the meal to welcome all the guests. A guest should wait to see if the host makes a toast before he makes one. Then if he wishes to propose a toast he must first ask permission of the host, and then only if it looks as though the host is not going to give one. The toast is more memorable if it is brief. A good rule of thumb is the age-old maxim KISS: Keep it short and simple. Remember, you're giving a toast, not a roast.

A toast is also appropriate during the dessert course when there is a guest of honor present. Before the guests eat their dessert, the host stands and makes the toast. Everyone drinks, except the guest of honor (it is considered bad form to drink to oneself). If you are in the honored spot, smile and refrain from touching your glass. When the host sits down, the guest of honor is expected to return the toast, and then he may drink.

Even if you don't drink alcohol you may still participate in a toast. You can toast with a nonalcoholic beverage or raise a glass of wine or champagne to your lips, pretend to drink, then set it aside.

Americans often find that liquor is a much bigger part of the business equation abroad than at home. In a country outside the United States, drinking alcohol may be as commonplace as drinking water. Dean Foster, president of Dean Foster Associates, a consulting firm that offers cross-cultural corporate training, says if you, as a foreign guest, refuse to drink, you may be sending a message that you don't trust the other person. "If you do not want to drink alcohol, the only surefire excuse is to claim that your doctor ordered you to lay off alcohol for a month," says Foster.

* * *

Although good etiquette is important in all business interactions, being a good host or guest is more than knowing how to wield a knife and fork correctly, when to toast, how to taste wine, or how to throw a successful party. A good host knows how to make their guests feel comfortable and can handle disasters with humor. A good guest knows how to converse with all kinds of people and can have a good time at any event, regardless of how formal or informal.

TIPS FROM THE TOP

Avoid messy and hard-to-eat foods in public.

Take care of the bill before your guests arrive.

Don't go to dinner hungry.

Meet for breakfast when you're short on time or money.

Respond promptly to all invitations.

If someone is toasting you, don't drink to yourself.

Chapter 7

TECHNO-ETIQUETTE: MINDING YOUR MANNERS IN THE ELECTRONIC AGE

> Technology is dominated by two types of people:
> those who understand what they do not manage, and
> those who manage what they don't understand.
>
> —SOURCE UNKNOWN

lame it on Alexander Graham Bell. With the patenting of the telephone in 1876, a new world of technology was born, bringing with it both blessings and curses. Technology is the essential link that allows us to communicate quickly and productively. With the proliferation of cell phones, pagers, e-mail, and other technological means, our business relationships are far less social than they once were. One of the many paradoxes of modern technology is that gadgets meant to connect us also isolate us. Because we can stay in touch regardless of where we are or what we're doing, face-to-face interactions have diminished to the point that strangers can complete multiple transactions without ever knowing what the other person looks or sounds like. Regardless of how much you rely on technology to communicate with clients, customers, or coworkers, you can still maintain the personal touch if you practice good techno-etiquette in the workplace.

HEAR NO EVIL: TELEPHONE COURTESIES THAT COUNT

Even though e-mail is the preferred method of communication for many of us, the telephone outranks e-mail in terms of expressing emotions and affection, giving advice, and providing companionship. This comes as no surprise, considering that the human voice carries a tremendous amount of emotional information that e-mail can't duplicate. If your voice is unfriendly or uncooperative, or if you give a person the impression that he is wasting your time, you may offend or intimidate him or encourage him to sever any business connections with you or your company. When callers are placed on hold for an eternity or don't receive return phone calls within a reasonable period of time, they get frustrated, hang up, or call your supervisor or, worse, one of your competitors.

While the telephone is one of the most often used pieces of technology, it is also one of the most often *misused*. At one time or another we've all been on the receiving end of unpardonable telephone manners. Several years ago my husband and I were renovating our bathroom and I called five glass companies to get quotes on a seamless shower door. Only three out of five called me back. Two companies called me the same day and the third called me four days later. I decided to hire the first company that responded to my call. In many cases, such as this one, I, like many others, make business decisions that aren't solely based on price. A company's reputation and fair price combined with a speedy response and a friendly telephone demeanor usually will win hands down.

telephone etiquette in the workplace

- When making a phone call, begin by identifying yourself and your company. If you are returning someone's call, include that information as well. Starting a conversation with "Hi, how ya doin'?" is much too personal and should not be used unless you know the person extremely well. (Besides, I've heard too many telemarketers use this phrase when they have called me.)

- When returning someone's phone call, consider their time zone so you don't call them before or after normal business hours. With so many people working from home these days, the phone call could awaken their family at an inconvenient time.

- Ask permission before putting someone on hold. "May I place you on hold while I connect you?" is more courteous than saying "Please hold." Also, if you leave callers on hold for an extended period of time without checking back in, they will become frustrated and aggravated, hang up, and then take their business elsewhere.

- Before transferring a call, give the name and extension of the person with whom the caller will be speaking. This information will be useful to the caller in the event you get disconnected.

- Long phone conversations can impede productivity, interfere with work, and delay appointments. If you find that a call is going nowhere or lingering longer than necessary, politely say something like, "Excuse me, Chris, I just noticed that I have another appointment right now. May I call you back or follow up with an e-mail?" This gentle hint will prompt the caller to get to the point and wind up the call.

- If a coworker walks into your office while you're on the phone, the caller takes priority unless the other person has an appointment. If the person who stepped in your office doesn't have an appointment, silently mouth the words "I'll call you when I finish" and then get back to him as soon as you end your phone conversation.

- If you have call waiting, refrain from answering another call when talking to your boss, customer, or client. If you're expecting an important call, let clients and coworkers know ahead of time before putting them on hold.

- Always return phone calls. Phone calls that are returned quickly can make the difference between winning or losing an important account or being chosen or passed up for a career opportunity. Not returning a phone call can make you appear aloof or make the caller feel unimportant. If you'd rather not do business with someone who repeatedly calls you, call after hours and leave them a message. Linda Kaplan Thaler, president of a multibillion-dollar advertising agency, attributes her successful career to something she calls "positive imprints"—the result of treating others in a positive, respectful way. "At our agency every phone call gets returned and every résumé gets a response," she says. Thaler feels this personal touch separates her company from those of her competitors.

speakerphones, voice mail, and fax machines

- Speakerphones are designed for conference calls. Always ask permission before putting someone on speakerphone. Not doing so could make the other person feel that her privacy is being violated.

- The one who initiates a conference call on a speakerphone is responsible for introducing all those who are participating. Participants should say their names before speaking so that others in the group can identify them.

- Don't use a speakerphone while working in a cubicle. Your loud conversations may interfere with nearby coworkers' concentration.

- If you suspect that you have been put on speakerphone and are uncomfortable with it, simply say, "I'm having difficulty hearing you. Would you mind taking me off your speakerphone?" The other person will generally pick up the handset immediately.

- When leaving a voice mail message, be brief. Slowly say your name and telephone number, followed by a message describing the nature of your call. It's helpful if you conclude the message by repeating your telephone number and the best time you can be reached. Repeating your number is especially important when calling from a cell phone, just in case the reception is poor and your voice fades without your knowledge.

- Keep your voice mail current and up-to-date. If you're going to be out of the office for an extended period of time, let callers know whom they can contact in your absence.

- To ensure that your fax reaches its destination, include a cover sheet containing the recipient's name, department, and company name; the number of pages; and your name and contact information.

- Call before faxing a multipage document. Lengthy documents use up a lot of ink in the recipient's fax machine and the recipient may prefer that you e-mail or send the document by mail instead.

- Don't send unsolicited advertisements through the fax machine. This is the same as sending spam over the Internet.

- When composing a fax, use a slightly larger font so the receiver can easily read your message.

COMMUNICATING ELECTRONICALLY WITHOUT LOSING THE PERSONAL TOUCH

E-mail is one of the most efficient ways of staying in touch with customers and clients. It's cheaper and faster than a letter, less intrusive than a phone call, less hassle than a fax, and often more convenient for the recipient. Because of these benefits, it has become the preferred method of communication for millions of executives around the world.

Keith Ferrazzi of Ferrazzi Greenlight says he uses e-mail as a relationship-maintenance tool to stay in touch with his clients. Ferazzi will set a reminder in his computer and then, whenever a friend or client celebrates a birthday or other special occasion, he will "ping" the person by sending a quick, casual greeting to acknowledge the event.

Katherine Catlin, founding partner of the Catlin & Cookman Group, a CEO consulting firm in Hingham, Massachusetts, says she and her colleagues use e-mail to introduce people who they think might benefit from meeting each other. "One of my former clients from Colorado recently sent a brief e-mail to me and to another person he thought I ought to meet. His opening greeting read, 'Dear Joe and Katherine: Joe Crawford, I'd like to introduce to you Katherine Catlin. She's a high-level thought leader in this area and has written two books on leadership for CEOs and can be reached at the number listed below. Katherine, Joe is the CEO of XYZ Company and is very interested in knowing more about your books and consulting services. He can be reached at the number listed below. Now ya'll take it from here.'" Catlin believes e-mail introductions such as this lead to valuable business connections that can go straight to the bottom line.

E-MAIL: HOW MUCH IS TOO MUCH?

Do you stare at a long queue of unread, unanswered e-mails on your screen every day? If so, you may be wondering how often you should use e-mail to stay in touch with colleagues and clients. At Intel Corporation, a study among eighty-eight thousand employees discovered that the average employee received approximately two hundred new e-mails a day, 30 percent of which were deemed unnecessary. With this amount of data overload, employees easily spend nearly three hours a day managing e-mail. It's always helpful to ask yourself, "Is this message necessary?" before you send it off to someone else's in-box. Whenever there is e-mail abuse, errors occur and stress is added to our immense workload. Also, given the prevalence of computer viruses and worms, think twice before you send along that hilarious attachment or latest joke. Be warned too that many companies have strict policies about the use of e-mail.

There are no set rules on how often you should send e-mail to clients, customers, or colleagues for it varies by industry, and even individually, since everyone has preferences in how to communicate. In general, e-mails should be used for simple matters, such as notification of when a contract arrives, scheduling an appointment, or following up on a previous conversation. More important issues, such as discussing contracts, proposals, or negotiations, and communications with new clients, are handled more effectively in person or by telephone.

NETIQUETTE: ELECTRONIC ETIQUETTE

Here are some points to keep in mind when e-mailing.

Use the subject line to inform. An e-mail's importance is often determined by its subject line. An e-mail without a subject is likely to be deleted. Keep the subject line brief, specific, and relevant, or else the receiver might mistake your e-mail for spam.

Treat e-mails like business letters. It's better to be more formal rather than too casual when you want to make a good impression. First, include a salutation such as "Dear Mr. Rodriguez," then focus on key points in the opening paragraph. Use the person's surname until he responds by signing his e-mail with his first name. This indicates that the person doesn't mind being addressed more casually. Most people prefer that you include a signature line containing your first and last name, title, company, and contact information. This is helpful in the event they need to contact you via phone or mail.

Don't shout. Using all UPPERCASE LETTERS is considered CYBER SHOUTING. As an alternative, use asterisks to emphasize key words: "Bob and I had a *wonderful* time at the company reception last night."

Skip the fancy decorations. Vivid colors, flashing symbols, or bouncing smiley faces (better known as "emoticons") are fun in personal e-mails but should be avoided in business communications.

Keep it brief, but not abrupt. Brevity is a must when sending e-mail, but sometimes you can be too brief and come across as being rude. Here is an example of how a short e-mail can be too short. My friend Rebecca once belonged to a professional association that prided itself on providing networking opportunities for its members. Because there was no membership director, Rebecca e-mailed the association president asking how she could contact another member she'd recently met. Three days went by and she still had not received a response. She e-mailed her request again, thinking that the first one had been lost somewhere in cyber limbo. The association president finally responded with only the e-mail address of the association member. Rebecca expected to get a more cordial response, such as "Dear Rebecca, my apologies for the delay. Sarah Reid's contact information is listed below. Please let us know if we can assist you further." Because the association president's e-mail was so abrupt, it made her appear rushed and rude.

No e-mail is private. If you wish to send someone confidential information, use the phone or meet in person. E-mails can be duplicated, forwarded, and printed, so don't send or say anything you wouldn't want repeated or posted in your company's newsletter.

Avoid mood mail. E-mail messages that convey strong emotion can easily be misinterpreted. E-mail should be avoided in potentially volatile circumstances, such as when firing or reprimanding someone or ending a contract; these situations are best handled in person. Never send an e-mail when you're angry. Take time to cool down, and reread the e-mail before you send it to be sure it doesn't contain anything you will regret later. Facial expression, vocal inflection, or body language isn't conveyed in an e-mail, so it's not uncommon for messages to be misconstrued as too harsh, too critical, or too casual. When you engage in face-to-face or voice-to-voice communication, it's easier to answer questions, clarify any possible misunderstandings, and preserve a mutual respect even if the business relationship is on shaky ground.

Praise in person. A congratulatory e-mail doesn't have the same impact as a personal thank-you note, no matter how many people you copy in the message. Besides, most people are likely to cherish typed or handwritten notes rather than e-mail messages.

Proof it before you send. It pays to check before you click. Before you hit the send button, check for grammar, spelling, and punctuation errors. The spell-check feature will not always catch words that are used out of context. For example, you may intend to type, "*They're* going to love our new product line." But by mistake you type, "*Their* going to love our new product line." Proofread your message to be sure it says what you want it to say and that all names are spelled correctly.

Respect others' privacy. There will be times when you need to deliver an e-mail to a large group but don't want to launch a massive distribution list by e-mailing everyone together. If the recipients are unacquainted and you don't want to divulge all addresses to all of the recipients, use the BCC (blind carbon copy) function. When BCC is used, the only other e-mail address that appears in the recipient's mailbox is that of the sender.

Be cautious about using the "Reply All" function. If you receive an e-mail that was sent to a multitude of people, including yourself, reply only to those who require a response. Hit "Reply All" only if it is crucial that every person on the distribution list see your response. In many cases, the sender is the only person who requires a response.

Don't be a pest. If you don't receive a response after sending an e-mail, either send a different e-mail explaining why you are following up, or pick up the phone if you need a prompt answer. Sending the same e-mail over and over again may make you appear pushy or impatient. Before you assume that your message was ignored or deleted by the receiver, know that most companies have anti-spam filters that may have accidentally blocked your e-mail.

Respond quickly. If someone e-mails you a question and you don't have an immediate answer, it's a courteous gesture to e-mail the sender to explain that you are researching their request or busy working on other projects at the moment and will get back to them within a certain time frame once you have the information. Otherwise, the person who e-mailed you may think their message never reached your in-box or that they are being ignored.

Send attachments only with permission. Many companies have policies discouraging employees from opening attachments from unknown sources. Before sending multiple attachments or photographs, find out if the receiver wants to receive them separately or collectively in one e-mail. Some people may choose to receive them separately so it doesn't slow down their other incoming e-mail messages.

Don't send unsolicited advertisements. Electronic newsletters are a great way to stay in touch with clients, coworkers, or colleagues and are an effective vehicle for promoting company news or new products and services. However, sending unsolicited e-mail advertisements isn't a smart business strategy when people are bombarded with hundreds of useless messages a week. To avoid being labeled a spammer, send e-mail newsletters and announcements only to those who have given you permission to do so. If someone chooses to "opt out," or be taken off your list, honor their request.

Think twice before sending humorous messages. A funny e-mail may seem innocent to you but may be insulting to someone else. E-mail messages that are hostile or harassing or carry discriminatory overtones are permanent and may be forwarded to others without your knowledge. Play it safe and don't send anything you wouldn't want posted in your company's newsletter.

Remember that less is more. For short e-mail, you can use the subject line only: "Can we meet this afternoon to go over budgets?" then finish the sentence with "(EOM)," the acronym for "end of message." The recipient won't need to open the message to respond. Use acronyms sparingly and only when your recipients know their meaning.

Mark your message "urgent" in other ways. As an alternative to the exclamation point, use a keyword at the beginning of the subject line to help recipients filter and sort time-sensitive e-mail quickly. For example, "Urgent" could be the code for "read immediately," while "FYI" could mean no response is required.

Tell others when you're not available. Use the "Out-of-Office" auto-respond feature if you plan to be out of the office for an extended period of time. Change your voice mail to notify callers when you are traveling, when you will return, and whom to contact in your absence.

Avoid unnecessary frustrations. Here are seven more ways e-mail users cause unnecessary frustration to others:

1. Using long signature files
2. Sending chain letters
3. Forgetting to send attachments
4. Sending virus hoaxes
5. Forgetting to check their e-mail regularly and having a full e-mail box
6. Not personalizing e-mail ("Dear Sir" is a dead giveaway that you didn't do your research)

7. Addressing someone by the wrong name or misspelling someone's name

BLACKBERRY DEVICES

Give clients, colleagues, and coworkers your full attention whenever you're in a meeting. Suppress the urge to doodle, tap your pen, chew ice, swivel, rock back and forth in your chair, sleep, clip your fingernails, or check e-mail on your BlackBerry. Jancee Dunn, a contributing editor for *Rolling Stone* and a writer for publications such as *O* magazine, says she gets frustrated when she conducts interviews with people who are more interested in checking their e-mail than in concentrating on the interview. "I have interviewed celebrities who are so preoccupied with their e-mail; they have the nerve to tap away on their BlackBerry while I'm trying to ask them questions," said Dunn.

If you are preoccupied with your e-mail device and do not give others your full attention, they are likely to take offense (and for good reason). Generally, e-mail devices should not be used in meeting environments because they take your focus off the speaker. I have read about companies that give periodic BlackBerry breaks during meetings so executives can check e-mail regularly. Under special circumstances, portable e-mail devices can be useful in meetings. For example, if you're waiting for an answer to a question you have posed to a client, scan the message headers and read only what is vital. Respond only if the matter can't wait until your meeting is over. Be discreet and apologize upfront if you think you might have to leave the room. Put the device on your belt or in your briefcase, or leave it in your office. If you put it on the table, you and others in the meeting may become distracted when it vibrates and alerts you that you've got mail.

CELL PHONES: A BLESSING AND A CURSE?

While cell phones make it easy to stay connected, they also distance us from the people who may be within earshot. Remember when phone booths had doors? They were designed to protect the caller's privacy. But a phone booth is a thing of the past, and so, apparently, is people's reluctance to discuss private matters in public places.

The population of wireless users continues to grow, and a survey released in 2004 by the Massachusetts Institute of Technology found that cell phones had surpassed alarm clocks, television sets, and answering machines as the invention people said they hated most but could not live without. How is it that a device most of us survived quite nicely without, as recently as a decade ago, now seems indispensable?

Cell phone misuse has provoked extreme irritation for many of us at one time or another. Where there's irritation, there's the probability that a business opportunity could be lost. In some instances, poorly timed cell phone use goes beyond rudeness—it alienates and angers those who are on the sidelines.

A couple of years ago, I experienced what I thought to be the most egregious cell phone offense. When I arrived for a scheduled massage, the therapist asked me to disrobe and lie face down on the massage table. After a few minutes she returned to the room, sat down on a stool, and began massaging my shoulders. I closed my eyes and started to relax. All of a sudden I felt her remove her right hand from my shoulder. She began talking. At first I thought another person had entered the room. I was shocked to discover that the massage therapist was talking on her cell phone to a friend. Her conversation went on for at least five minutes as she massaged me with one hand. After she hung up, she apologized to me, but I didn't respond because I was so shocked at her behavior. In retrospect, I wish I had refused to pay for the massage, but instead I simply decided to take my business elsewhere.

BUSINESSES ARE ENCOURAGING CELL PHONE COURTESY

More businesses are jumping on the bandwagon to help combat rude cell phone behavior but progress is slow. Movie theaters post SILENCE IS GOLDEN signs, airline clubs have signs that designate quiet areas, and Amtrak, the transportation giant, even has "Quiet Cars," where customers are asked to refrain from using cell phones, pagers, or the sound feature of laptop computers, and to speak only in subdued tones. If someone sits in a Quiet Car and uses her cell phone, the conductor will politely escort her to a seat in another car.

Sprint released a Wireless Courtesy Report in July 2004 that revealed an overwhelming majority of Americans admitted to knowing proper cell phone etiquette but did not always practice it. Of the respondents, 40 percent admitted to discussing private issues in public places and 77 percent had overheard cell phone calls in public restrooms. Overall, 80 percent said they felt people were less courteous when using a cell phone today than five years ago. However, 97 percent of those surveyed classified themselves as "very courteous" or "somewhat courteous" when they used a cell phone.

The proliferation of cell phone abuse led me to create National Cell Phone Courtesy Month several years ago. Every July, I speak to as many people as I can about cell phone etiquette and its importance in our professional and personal lives. I consider cell phone rudeness a social disease that isn't going to be cured anytime soon. If we ignore this rudeness problem, stress and anxiety will continue to escalate. But I'm hopeful that, in time, cell phone etiquette education will breed awareness and awareness will breed solutions.

eight tips for becoming a more courteous cell phone user

1. *Cute, quirky ring tones are not appropriate in every setting.* Although specialized ring tones allow you to express your personality and differentiate your ringing phone from others, they can be be annoying in certain settings. Set your phone to silent, vibrate, or on a standard ring tone when you are in a business setting or public area where others could get annoyed.

2. *Let your voice mail take your calls.* Refrain from taking calls during religious services, job interviews, golf outings, movies, funerals, classes, business meetings, public performances, or in restaurants and courtrooms. Of course, there are exceptions to every rule. If you are a physician on call, an expectant father, or a parent waiting for a child or babysitter to call, alert your clients, coworkers, or companions ahead of time and step away when the call comes in.

3. *The people you are with should take precedence over calls you want to make or receive.* Poor cell phone etiquette can have a negative impact on how your friends, clients, or coworkers view your re-

lationship with them. People may feel disrespected or ignored and perhaps think you don't value them or their time if you take calls while in their company. Turn your phone off, put it on vibrate, and let your voice mail take your calls. If you are expecting a call that can't be postponed, alert your companions ahead of time. Excuse yourself, step away, and keep the call brief.

4. *If you can't be out of touch, use the options your cell phone provides to stay connected without offending others.* Many cell phones have a one-button feature that turns off the ringer to prevent disruptions. Other features, such as text messaging, wireless e-mail, voice mail, caller ID, and distinctive ringing, are designed to help you receive messages or stay connected without disturbing those around you.

5. *Be courteous to those within hearing distance.* Use discretion when discussing private matters or sensitive business topics in front of others. Matters such as medical exams, torrid love affairs, personal arguments, or deals gone bust should be discussed in private.

6. *Don't be guilty of "cell yell."* It's not necessary to speak louder than normal for callers to hear you. Conversations that are likely to be emotional should be held where they will neither embarrass nor intrude on others. According to the 2004 Sprint Wireless Courtesy Report, almost nine out of ten Americans (88 percent) think people raise their voices unnecessarily when speaking on a cell phone; while only 15 percent of those surveyed say they personally have been told they talk too loud on their cell phone.

7. *Don't be a cell phone cop.* If you encounter someone talking too loudly on a cell phone, don't take matters into your own hands. Walk away, change locations if possible, or find someone in a position of authority to address the situation. If you must confront a cell phone

offender, do it discreetly and diplomatically. You might, for example, say, "Excuse me, would you mind keeping your voice down? I'm having trouble hearing the speaker. Thank you."

8. *Make safety your most important call.* Practice wireless responsibility while driving. Don't make or answer calls while in heavy traffic or facing hazardous driving conditions. Use a hands-free device in order to increase your safety.

CAMERA PHONES

Camera phones are extremely popular. Most people take pictures with them just for fun, others use their camera phone pictures as a means to send pictures of projects to clients. But some people have used the photo capability to invade the privacy of others, and this is not only rude but illegal. As with any camera, ask permission before taking anyone's picture. In extreme circumstances, ignoring that rule can lead to criminal prosecution.

PUSH-TO-TALK PHONES

Push-to-talk phones, or walkie-talkie-type phones, are designed to let you contact someone immediately without having to dial or look up their phone number. These phones can be distracting when someone hears both sides of your conversation. Keep your voice down when using one of these devices or turn off the walkie-talkie speaker and listen through the earpiece.

Technology is revolutionizing the business arena in much the same way the Wright Brothers revolutionized the aviation industry. Yet new technology can raise more questions about etiquette and manners than it answers. Technology can help save time and increase productivity, but it can also create new challenges and frustrations. By practicing techno-etiquette, you will have a distinct advantage over others and will be able to use technology the way it was intended—to enhance communication and project a more professional image.

TIPS FROM THE TOP

Treat your e-mail as you would a business letter.

Cool down before sending a hot e-mail.

Return phone calls within twenty-four hours.

When talking on a cell phone, speak in a low voice and don't discuss private matters in public.

Use speakerphones for conference calls only.

Chapter 8

GOING GLOBAL: HOW TO AVOID AN INTERNATIONAL INCIDENT

A traveler of taste will notice that the wise are polite
all over the world, but the fool only at home.

—OLIVER GOLDSMITH,

playwright and novelist

My mother has a saying, "Your life can change in an
instant with one phone call or one trip to the
post office." My life changed in February 1993
when Northwest Airlines' Crew Scheduling called me at my
apartment in Boston. The purpose? To inform me about a trip I
was not ready to take. "Jacqueline, please report to work tomorrow
evening at five-thirty p.m. You're going to Saudi Arabia." I
couldn't believe my ears. Saudi Arabia? Never in my wildest
dreams did I imagine I would ever get to go to such an exotic
place. Northwest Airlines was sending a military charter plane to
pick up a load of servicemen and servicewomen, and I was chosen
to be part of the flight crew. How could I possibly prepare for
such a trip with just one day's notice? Dutifully I packed my suit-

case and hoped for the best. Little did I know that my lack of preparation would cause me much embarrassment.

When our flight crew arrived in the city of Dhahran, we checked into our hotel. Much to my surprise, each female flight attendant was given a room key and an abaya—a floor-length black garment. We were advised to wear it over our clothing whenever we went out in public. We were also asked to wear a head scarf. As it turned out, only two women had packed a scarf, and I wasn't one of them. If I'd had the time to do a little research on the local culture, or if my company had provided some cross-cultural training, I would have been better prepared.

Tired from traveling, I couldn't wait to go to my room and get some sleep. When I got off the elevator and turned the first corner, I froze in my tracks and let out a gasp. I found myself facing four Saudi Arabian women dressed in black from head to toe. I couldn't even see their faces, which were veiled. I had never seen women dressed this way. They must have been surprised to see me too, because they also stopped and let out a big gasp. Had I had the luxury of lead time for this trip, I would have experienced less shock, awkwardness, and stress. The next morning, our group was assigned a guide to take us sightseeing and shopping. I was surprised to learn that women could not go out in public without a male escort. As naïve as I was, I had a wonderful time getting acquainted with Middle Eastern culture. Since that visit, I have not returned to Saudi Arabia, but I still relish the memories and the lessons I learned along the way.

Lack of preparation seems to be a shortcoming for most U.S. executives who conduct business overseas. Very few people take the time to do their homework so they can learn how to interact comfortably with people of other cultures. Executives from other countries, on the other hand, often spend substantial time and money researching U.S. business and social customs. For example, a friend of mine who works for a large fruit packing plant in Lake Wales, Florida, tells me when the Japanese businessmen visit her company, they know as much about the citrus industry as she does.

DEVELOP A GLOBAL MIND-SET

To stay competitive in our ever-changing business climate, cultural competence and a global mind-set are musts. Roger Axtell, author of *Do's and Taboos of Hosting International Visitors,* defines a successful global executive as someone who practices "chameleon management." In other words, this person possesses the ability and willingness to adapt to the colorations and textures of other cultures, adjusting to the client's culture and way of doing business. If you can do this, you can turn differences into opportunities and create success in situations where others are left with embarrassment and failure.

Mountain climber Stacy Allison learned that taking preconceived ideas, notions, and stereotypes into a new business relationship doesn't work. You have to go in with a clean slate and be willing to listen and learn. Allison learned this lesson more than fifteen years ago when her climbing team arrived in Katmandu. "We had just landed at the airport," she told me, "and we were eager to retrieve our four hundred sixty boxes of food and equipment from customs so we could begin our journey to climb Mount Everest. In fact, we were so eager that we didn't bother knocking on the customs agent's door. We burst through.

" 'Namaste,' said the agent.

" 'Namaste,' we responded. 'We would like our gear.'

"The customs agent asked us to sit down, but we just looked at one another. We had just endured a seventeen-hour flight to Katmandu and the last thing we wanted to do was sit again.

" 'No, thank you, we would like to get our gear, please,' we said.

" 'You must come back this afternoon at two-thirty,' he said. 'Your paperwork is not ready.'

"We turned around and left, knowing we had many other things to do before we could begin our expedition. But we returned to the customs agent's office once again at two-thirty and burst through his door.

" 'Namaste,' he said. 'Please sit.'

"This time we did, and we were surprised when he ordered tea. Tea? How could he not understand that we had more important things to do than to sit and drink tea? 'No, thank you,' we said. 'Could we please get our gear?'

" 'Your paperwork still is not ready. You must come back tomorrow at eight-thirty a.m.,' he said. So we left.

"The next day, in we came and out we went—a pattern that went on for seven days. It finally dawned on us that we were doing something wrong. We hadn't taken the time to learn local customs and what was expected of us."

Allison acknowledges that she and her team were so caught up in their own agenda that they completely missed what was going on. All they could think about was climbing the mountain. She and her team had thought they were running the show, but in reality the customs agent was in charge. Because of their stubbornness and lack of cultural awareness, this lesson cost Allison and her team eleven days and a gift of two thousand dollars before they learned their lesson and could get their hands on their precious gear.

PUT RELATIONSHIPS FIRST

Americans who are deal-oriented believe time is money. It is not uncommon for two U.S. executives to greet, shake hands, start discussing business in the first five minutes of conversation, get the deal signed, and then leave. Socializing and idle chitchat are often perceived as a waste of time. But executives in other regions, such as Asia, Latin America, and the Middle East, put a premium on relationship protocol. In other words, they place a great deal of importance on trust and respect, which takes time and patience to develop. For example, in Japan you may be invited to tea several times before someone decides whether or not to do business with you. If a person likes you, business eventually follows. In South America, you may spend the first hour or two getting acquainted with a colleague and then be given a tour of the city, including a visit to a local site, followed by lunch. This provides an opportunity for the client to get to know you and your company better.

INTERNATIONAL-RELATIONSHIP-SKILL BUILDING

More than a decade ago, high-tech skills were highly marketable. Today, with more companies going global and becoming more multicultural, the ability to connect and relate with people from different backgrounds is equally essential whether you're traveling overseas to do business or working with colleagues in the United States who are from a variety of different countries.

Be observant and ask questions. When traveling internationally, notice how people act, dress, and treat each other. If you come from a culture that emphasizes verbal communication, try to be aware of messages that are conveyed without words. When you can interpret a situation correctly, you improve your ability to fit in. If you are unable to interpret what's going on, you can still learn a great deal simply by being alert and watching those around you. For example, does your international client or colleague put his hands in his lap or does he rest his wrists on the edge of the table during dinner? Does he eat with the fork constantly in his left hand? How does he signal a server? If you don't understand why someone does something a certain way or says something unfamiliar, ask. Many people don't want to reveal how little they know about other cultures, so they don't ask questions and they muddle through. Questions show you have an interest in a person's culture and help build your relationship. People will generally forgive your blunders if they know you are making an effort to learn about their culture. However, if your behavior is indifferent or arrogant, they will be less tolerant or unforgiving.

Think before you speak. We all know that lines of communications weaken and misunderstandings are apt to take place when people don't share the same language. Translators are worth their weight in gold when delicate business negotiations are at stake. If you use an interpreter to communicate with a person from another country, look at and speak directly to that person instead of the interpreter. If you don't use an interpreter, stick to simple and direct language. Humor is subjective and some jokes or slang expressions don't translate well. This can cause confusion or offense. Stay away from controversial subjects like politics and religion, unless, of course, your host brings up the subjects.

Keep an open mind. Minds are like parachutes and umbrellas, they function only when open. When you visit a client or colleague's country, adjust your style of business to fit his. Years ago, while employed by a hotel, I worked with a colleague who used to irritate the rest of us in our department by stating, "It's my way or the highway." Sadly, his way *was* the only way and he was reluctant to consider anyone else's ideas. Those who travel overseas with the intent of conducting business the same way they do business at home are in for a rude awakening. As stated earlier, it's to your advantage to research other cultures and business practices before you pack your bags or welcome international visitors to the United States.

Be aware that something as simple as a handshake differs from culture to culture. In the United States, short, firm handshakes are used to communicate confidence and self-assurance, while in other places, handshakes may be lighter or linger a bit longer. In the United States, direct eye contact is a way of showing interest in the other person. In other countries, eye contact may be kept to a minimum as a way of showing deference or respect. Americans tend to be very direct—we like to think we say what we mean and mean what we say. Yet there are other cultures, particularly Asian cultures, that are indirect in their communication styles. For example, if an Asian client nods his head up and down, it doesn't necessarily mean that he agrees with you. Nodding is a form of acknowledgment.

Be available to assist. Every time you step on international soil, you become a guest of that country. Your business hosts will probably do everything they can to make you feel welcome and comfortable. Don't be surprised if your international counterpart personally picks you up from the airport, escorts you to some local attractions, or takes you to his home for dinner.

When your international counterpart comes to the United States, reciprocate with the same kind of warm hospitality. If you are unable to pick your guest up at the airport, arrange for someone of similar rank and status to greet him. Sending a cab or limousine service to pick up your special visitor doesn't convey the same feeling of welcome and may be interpreted as impersonal or uncaring.

Roger Axtell learned this lesson the hard way. "On one occasion," he says, "I hired a limousine service to pick up very important guests from Buenos Aires, who spoke very little English. They were unfamiliar with Chicago's O'Hare International Airport, they were arriving after a long, tiring overnight flight, and they had no idea how to find transportation to my office, more than one hundred miles away. It was essential to have someone meet them. Although the hired driver had the flight and gate number and arrival time, he came back empty-handed, saying meekly, 'I just couldn't find them.' I learned later that my guests sat in the baggage area for three hours, assuming the driver had been delayed.

"Because it was a weekend, they couldn't telephone our office, so they finally located a Spanish-speaking individual, who helped them find the bus service to our city. Topping off this misadventure, I later learned that the day of their arrival also happened to be the birthday of the senior visitor. It was a hosting nightmare."

Appreciate the differences. Travel with an open mind when visiting countries that are less abundant than your own. If you compare living standards in the United States with those of your international hosts, you could create an immediate barrier. There's nothing wrong with being proud of where you live, but boasting and comparing can be counterproductive to establishing a successful relationship.

When you're in a public place where everyone speaks another language, it's easy to forget that those around you may well speak and understand English. When traveling, it would be wise to avoid making comparisons and negative comments. While riding a train in Italy several years ago, I overhead an American teenager telling his friend that he liked the pizza in America more than he liked the pizza in Italy. While it was a fairly innocent comment, I was embarrassed for him because he didn't realize there were others on the train who understood every word of his conversation.

Be apprised of world events. Real estate magnate Donald Trump is successful in selling and renting apartments to people of many nationalities because he understands how other cultures operate on a business level. In his book *Trump: How to Get Rich*, he writes, "I have always lived in the United States, but I make an effort to be informed about other cultures. We're very much up to snuff about our own national events, but we are less aware of what's happening in other countries."

Keep abreast of world events by reading the newspaper, watching the news, and listening to talk radio. You don't have to be an expert in international affairs, but it's helpful to know the basics, like what foods your visitors or hosts enjoy, what holidays are observed in their country, and a little bit about their government. In many countries, for example, talking about your hosts' favorite sport could put you in a good light.

Notice nonverbal cues. Americans tend to be uncomfortable with silence. But in some countries, silence is used as a negotiation tool or a way to regroup thoughts. Nonverbal communication, like body language and facial expressions, often speaks louder than any words you could use. Watch international clients and colleagues closely and look for what isn't being said. If you talk much and listen little, you may miss some valuable information.

Acquaint yourself with different eating habits. If your international hosts invite you to dinner while you are visiting their country, observe how they eat and don't pass judgment. Observe how other guests ask for more food and how they signal when they have had enough. What may be considered bad form in the United States may be common practice in another country. For example, in Japan, as in Hong Kong, slurping is not considered rude. Instead, it is a sign of approval and appreciation for the cooking. Such noises should be interpreted as a compliment and not bad manners.

The act of cleaning one's plate has different meanings too, depending on the culture. In Thailand, leaving food means that you are finished or the food was delicious. In the Cambodian culture, if you clean your plate, it means you still want more and the hosts haven't provided enough to eat. In Japan, cleaning your plate means you appreciate the food.

If you are hosting a dinner for international visitors, be sure to serve foods that are not taboo. For example, Muslims and Jews don't eat pork and Hindus don't eat beef. Muslims, Hindus, Mormons, and members of some Protestant sects do not drink alcoholic beverages.

Learn a few phrases. Learn at least a few common phrases before traveling abroad or welcoming international visitors to the United States. Your efforts will be appreciated. When Barbara Corcoran of the Corcoran Group was asked to speak to a gathering of thirty-five Japanese businessmen back in the 1980s, she immediately saw a potential business opportunity. Corcoran bought a Japanese phrase book and memorized a few phrases, including the words for "Thank you for coming and listening and I hope you will come back soon." Corcoran says, "When I got to the microphone and said my first line in Japanese, everyone in the room smiled at me and nodded. There was a translator who translated everything else. At the end of my speech, my audience members all came up to me, bowed, and presented me with their business cards. As a result of my efforts, I ended up selling more New York condos to the Japanese than any of my competitors."

Begin by using surnames and professional titles. In the United States we are very informal in many business situations and we tend to operate on a first-name basis. However, instant familiarity doesn't always make a favorable impression in other parts of the world. Wait until the client or colleague lets you know when it is acceptable to use her first name. Addressing someone by their correct title conveys respect. A title such as "doctor" or "professor" is highly valued in Germany, Italy, and many other countries. It takes years to attain an advanced degree or specialized skills and it's courteous to acknowledge that status.

Give the appropriate gift. Gift-giving customs can be tricky if you don't do your research. Did you know, for example, that in China giving an expensive gift may be interpreted as a bribe? Or that in the Middle East gifts are exchanged with the right hand because the left hand is reserved for hygiene?

Kate Berardo, creator of a Web site dedicated to cultural awareness (*www.culturosity.com*) and—with Simma Lieberman and George Simons—coauthor of *Putting Diversity to Work,* says she learned the intricacies of gift-giving when she worked for a Japanese company several years ago. Berardo purchased sets of stationery for her manager and five of her coworkers, thinking the nicely wrapped gifts would be appropriate. Although Berardo knew gift-giving played an important role in the Japanese culture, she didn't realize that when she gave the same gift to everyone, she was sending a message that everyone was equal. In essence, she wasn't showing respect to her manager's rank and status. "Hierarchy and status should be observed at all times," Berardo told me. "I learned that respect is shown in the way you bow, how you speak, what you give, and the manner in which you present gifts."

Try it, you might like it. When you are the guest of honor in another country, you may be served a local delicacy, like duck tongue, cow stomach, or pickled jellyfish, for dinner. Your hosts may even wait for you to take a bite before they begin eating. If you aren't sure what you've been served, smile and try it anyway. If you leave it on your plate without trying it, you may insult your host. Eat what you can and move the rest of it around on your plate so it looks as if you've eaten more of it. Martha Rogers, Ph.D., of Peppers & Rogers Group says if you are served something unfamiliar, go ahead and eat it and, if possible, enjoy it. "Nine times out of ten, I have actually enjoyed eating things I didn't think I would like," says Rogers. "In Spain, I was served what appeared to be delicious noodles, then I found out that they were baby eels. I was the only one at the table served eels because they are so expensive and are considered a delicacy. I actually liked them. In Mexico City, I was served fried grubs. I ate them and discovered that they weren't bad. They were fried in garlic and tasted somewhat like Chee·tos. Whenever you're served something strange, say to yourself that millions of people have eaten these things for thousands of years and survived. I can too."

Learn the appropriate greeting. The question of physical

contact is one of the great imponderables of international business dealings. The rules on whom to touch, where to touch, and when, why, for how long, and with what degree of enthusiasm to touch vary from country to country. In the Dominican Republic, a kiss on the cheek is a common greeting among friends. In France, friends greet each other with a peck on both cheeks. A kiss on the cheek is becoming a more prevalent greeting in the multicultural workplace. If an international client or colleague greets you with a kiss, follow suit. You might offend the person if you step back or try to pull away. There's no need to take offense at a person's style of greeting as long as it's in good taste and you know the person well. If you're not sure how to greet an international visitor or client, start with a handshake or follow the person's lead.

Practice patience. Working with people from other cultures may require patience on occasion. Communication will be slowed when you work with someone who has an altogether different concept of time. Expect most things to take longer than they would in your own country. Decision-making styles differ around the globe. While American managers usually make decisions by themselves, Japanese managers tend to make decisions by consensus, a practice that adds time to the negotiation process. "Americans value flexibility. On the other hand, once a Japanese manager has reached a decision, he believes it is shameful to change it," reports Mitsugu Iwashita, director of the Intercultural and Business Communications Center, a Tokyo-based management consulting firm. Patience is the key to successful business negotiations.

Avoid making gestures. Gestures do not have universal meanings. A gesture that is commonly used in the United States could be misunderstood or considered insulting in other countries. The co-owner of a Latin-American restaurant in Washington, D.C., once told me he made a serious snafu while on a buying trip in Salvador, Brazil. One day while dining with one of his international clients, he noticed some local patrons giving a thumbs-up sign to waiters to show their appreciation for the food. He then demonstrated to his client how the A-OK sign is given to show appreciation in the United States. Horrified and embarrassed, the client told him that the gesture he had just made was highly offensive in Brazil. Fortunately for him, the client forgave him for his lack of knowledge. The less you rely on gestures to communicate your message, the more confident and sophisticated you will appear.

Expect the unexpected. Even the best-laid plans and the best intentions can go awry if you don't study a person's culture before traveling to another country or hosting international visitors. Be ready to engage in an alternative if your original plan doesn't work out as expected. On her first trip to Japan, Martha Rogers, Ph.D., of the Peppers & Rogers Group, learned that signing a person's name in red ink can be a major faux pas. "I was at a book signing and I used a red ink pen to sign one of my books and then gave it to a Japanese patron. Little did I know that some Asian cultures never sign a person's name in red unless it's for a deceased person or at the anniversary of a death," says Rogers. "Although he kindly called it to my attention, he said he didn't mind. I quickly apologized, took it back, then I bought him another book and signed it in black. Since then I always try to take the time to learn the little things that might offend someone in another country."

Find the humor. Travel can be stressful, so use humor to help you through difficult situations. Be able to step away (at least mentally) from situations and laugh at yourself from time to time.

Humor can interrupt embarrassment and bond you with an international client, colleague, or visitor.

Roger Axtell shared this story of how a team of U.S. executives from a helicopter-manufacturing company experienced a comedy of errors while hosting some Chinese counterparts several years ago:

"The large helicopter-manufacturing company prepared an elaborate, multicourse dinner for their Chinese guests, complete with chopsticks and fortune cookies. When the Chinese sat down, they picked up the knives and forks, while all the Americans picked up their chopsticks. After dinner, one of the Chinese guests started eating his fortune cookie and for several minutes he sat there while the slip of paper containing his fortune protruded from his mouth." Unbeknownst to the Americans, the fortune cookie was invented by a Los Angeles noodle manufacturer in 1916 and fortune cookies were virtually unknown to Asians until 1993, when the Wonton Food Company opened a factory in China.

Knowledge builds self-confidence. Before you embark on your next trip overseas or before you greet international visitors who will be visiting you in the United States, go to a library or bookstore or go online to learn more about a particular country and culture. Check out *www.executiveplanet.com* to find free information on business dress, topics of conversation, gift giving, entertaining, negotiating, and more. At *www.culturegrams.com* you can purchase pamphlets on the customs and geography of 180 countries. Each CultureGram contains information regarding greetings, eating habits, gestures, holidays, religion, events, trends, and more.

It's beneficial to your job success to learn about behavior, courtesies, comportment, and protocol before doing business overseas or hosting or "relating to" international visitors. You'll be more at ease knowing what potential blunders to avoid so you don't ruin a deal or a professional relationship. You'll also be more aware and open-minded, and this, in turn, will help you gain a competitive edge in the global economy.

TIPS FROM THE TOP

Don't be afraid to ask questions.

Tailor your business style to each particular culture when traveling overseas.

Know what's going on outside your own backyard.

Try foods that are foreign to you.

Refrain from using first names without permission.

The American way is not the only way. Keep an open mind.

Chapter 9

THE POWER OF POSITIVE THANKING

Gratitude is the most exquisite form of courtesy.
—JACQUES MARITAIN,
French philosopher

When was the last time you received a handwritten thank-you note? Perhaps it's easier to remember the last time you expected to receive one but didn't. "I'm too busy" is an all-too-popular excuse for not sending thank-you notes these days. As children, we were taught the importance of writing a thank-you note to anyone who gave us a present or did something special for us. As adults, the gifts we receive aren't all tangible, but they can cost us a heavy price if we fail to say thanks. Whenever someone gives you their time, advice, or a helping hand, that's reason enough to express your gratitude.

Al Ries, best-selling author and chairman of Ries & Ries, a marketing consulting firm in Atlanta, says neglecting to say thank you is one of the single biggest problems in the world today. "It's easy to criticize when things don't get done or when something is forgotten, but for many people, it's difficult remembering to offer a kind word when something nice happens, says Ries. And Hal Urban, in his best-selling book *Life's Greatest Lessons,* writes, "Whether it's a general decline in good manners or the attitude of many people that they're entitled to service and special attention from others, we don't hear that special phrase as much as we used to."

A mere 10 percent of employees report they have supervisors who say a daily thank you for a job well done, according to a recent nationwide Maritz poll. More than half of employees say they never, seldom, or only occasionally get thanked. Yet showing appreciation for others is one of the highest expressions of respect and courtesy we can offer. It's also one of the surest ways to make connections, strengthen emotional ties, and forge friendships and business relationships.

SAYING THANK YOU ENHANCES YOUR MARKETABILITY

Donald Trump says writing thank-you notes can impact your bottom line. In an e-mail to me, he wrote, "Not only will people remember that you took the time to write, they will also consider you thoughtful, responsible, and aware. These are good attributes to have in business."

According to a survey commission by Robert Half International, 76 percent of business executives take into account post-interview thank-you notes when evaluating job candidates. Unfortunately, only 36 percent of candidates send them. A well-written note could increase the chance of getting your foot in a company's door or give you an edge over other competitors vying for the same account. "Thank-you notes have become so rare that they are one of the simplest, most direct ways for a person to stand out and be one-of-a-kind instead of one-of-many," says author Sam Horn.

Years ago, I wrote three memorable thank-you notes which helped me land a much-sought-after position at the Breakers. When I interviewed for a position as a publicist with the resort, I was required to meet with the director of sales, the director of public relations, and the hotel president. During my interviews, I observed how each person's office was decorated. On entering the sales director's office, I immediately noticed his well-worn set of Ping golf clubs propped up in the corner. His golf tournament trophies and photos were displayed on the credenza. It was obvious he loved to play golf. The hotel president's walls were adorned with pictures of polo ponies, so I concluded that he liked the game of polo. The director of public relations had a set of small black-and-white porcelain cows situated near her telephone.

"Do you like cows?" I asked.

"Yes, I do," she replied.

Following my interviews, I went to the mall and looked for a card featuring horses and another with golf balls. I then wrote a nice note on each and mailed them to the hotel president and the director of sales. For the director of public relations I purchased a plain white five-by-seven-inch puzzle. With colored markers I wrote on the puzzle, "Let me solve your puzzled mind by providing the missing piece." On one puzzle piece I signed my name. Along with the puzzle, I expressed my thanks on a piece of stationery adorned with a couple of cartoon cows riding in a convertible. I inserted the puzzle and thank-you note in an envelope and sealed it. Then I tied four colored helium balloons to the envelope and sent it by courier to the public relations director's office. She was so impressed with my effort and originality she called the next day to thank me. A week later I was hired.

A thank-you note doesn't have to be as elaborate as the ones I wrote to the three executives at the Breakers. In that particular situation, I felt I would have more of a competitive edge if the notes were tailored to fit the personalities of those who interviewed me. After all, I was applying for a creative-minded position. In most situations, a thank-you note should be short, simple, and meaningful. Thank-you notes may be written for any occasion—after meeting with an important client, after an interview with a prospective employer, when you receive a gift, or when you're invited to dinner. The following are some strategies to consider when writing your next thank-you note.

Write by hand. When a client or someone you work with does something especially nice or goes out of his way for you, there is no substitute for a handwritten note. This personal touch will convey that you cared enough to take the time to sit down and think about that person. If you think your handwriting is barely legible, print. It takes just a few moments to write a brief thank-you note and there is a thousand-to-one return when you take the time to express your gratitude. People remember a thank you long after they have forgotten what they did for you.

Invest in good-quality stationery. Every executive should have a supply of personal and business stationery on hand at all times. Rather than buying generic note cards with "Thank You" printed on them, consider purchasing a set of premium correspondence cards with your name or company name elegantly engraved. One way some people determine the quality of your product or service is by looking at the quality of stationery you use.

Keep it short. Thank-you notes don't have to be long and laborious. Three or four carefully crafted sentences are usually enough to get the point across. In your note, mention something specific about the event or gift. Here is an example: "Thank you for referring ABC Corporation to me. I had my first consultation with the president and everything went smoothly. In fact, he plans to use several of my products in the near future. I truly appreciate your confidence in me. Thank you again."

Send it to the right person, properly addressed. When writing a thank-you note, it's bad form to misspell a person's name or address her by the wrong name or title. To be sure you have the correct information, get a business card before you leave, make a quick phone call to the company's receptionist, or visit the person's Web site. James R. Lucas of Luman Consultants International recalls the time a job applicant's forgetfulness eliminated her chances of working with his company. Lucas says the candidate addressed him and his assistant by the wrong names in her thank you note. "This was telltale evidence that this applicant didn't take the time to get the details right," says Lucas. "It was an etiquette disaster that resulted despite her good intentions."

Send it promptly. A thank-you note shows more than good manners. When you send a note within one or two days after a coworker, client, or customer does something special for you, it showcases your sincerity. Even if you feel that too much time has lapsed, send a thank-you note anyway. You're better off sending it late than never.

Keep the personal touch. While the importance of saying thank you hasn't changed, advances in technology have raised questions of how thank-you notes are best delivered. A thank-you call is appropriate in some casual circumstances and e-mail is better than nothing at all. But save these methods for when the situation is informal. Thank-you notes sent via e-mail have less impact for the same reason that makes them attractive—they require little time and effort.

Barbara Corcoran says handwritten notes carry three times the weight of an e-mail thank you. "With an e-mail you get the feeling it was sent on the fly, whereas with a handwritten note, you know someone stopped what they were doing and took the time to remember you," says Corcoran. Whenever you send an electronic thank you, keep in mind that the recipient might delete your note by mistake or your note might be intercepted by the company's spam filter and never reach its destination.

Today, small niceties such as thank-you notes give you a competitive advantage. A Lenox etiquette survey showed that few people express appreciation anymore. Nearly five out of every ten people surveyed said they don't always say thanks. Remembering to show your gratitude, either with a handwritten note or a small gift, can lead to better relationships that could eventually turn into opportunities.

Pat Williams of the Orlando Magic says an attitude of gratitude is vital in all professions. "Thank-you notes and meaningful gifts are kept and never forgotten," says Williams. "If I get a nice letter, it goes into a file. I don't throw it away."

Neil Cavuto, business news anchor with FOX News, told me he writes a minimum of ten to fifteen thank-you notes a day. "Little things can get big results," says Cavuto. "It's part of my day. It's like working out." Cavuto says that in the television business, a thank-you note is a way to get guests to come back. "In the early days before my show was well known, I would personally call or write CEOs and invite them to come on the show. I've continued this tradition ever since." Today, Cavuto receives notes from guests who tell him they've never received a thank you note from a television host before.

Jack Mitchell of the Mitchells/Richards clothing stores in Connecticut, says thank-you notes are the heart of his company's success. "My mind-set is that my client or customer is a friend," says Mitchell. "Between the months of September and December, I send more than thirteen hundred thank-you notes to our top customers. If writing thank-you notes starts at the top, then all your employees will see the value in writing them."

Gift-giving is a wonderful way of expressing your gratitude, in addition to writing thank-you notes. But beware: if you plan to give a gift, be sure to research a company's gift policy before you spend. Some companies have restrictions on the amount a client or employee may receive. Also, be careful when giving superiors at your own company a gift. Gifts that are too personal or too expensive could be perceived as a bribe or as "kissing-up." In the event you give the boss or company president something, it's best to have it come from a group of coworkers or your entire department. If you work for a very small company and feel you must give your boss a gift, don't go overboard and buy something extravagant. Most people enjoy small luxuries like books, music, or coffee. A gift card to your boss's favorite bookstore or coffee shop or a CD by her favorite artist will be appreciated.

According to a study from the University of California, Davis, just thinking about what you're grateful for can increase your happiness. Chief researcher Robert Emmons explains that gratitude fosters positive emotions that in turn boost your immune system. Regardless of how you choose to say thank you, you'll be healthier for having done it.

More on Thank-You Notes

- *Whenever a client, coworker, or colleague does something extraordinarily nice for you or gives you a gift, send a handwritten thank-you note within forty-eight hours.*
- *Acknowledge small favors with a telephone call or e-mail.*
- *Write a business thank-you note on a good-quality correspondence card. A personal thank-you note may be written on a card purchased from a specialty store or gift shop. Crane & Company (www.crane.com) carries a wide variety of elegant stationery that can be personalized for business or personal correspondence.*
- *Keep your thank-you note short. Three or four sentences will suffice.*
- *Never use a postage meter when sending thank-you notes. Use an attractive stamp instead.*
- *If your handwriting is poor, hand-print your message. A computer-generated thank-you note is more impersonal. Besides, there's no way for the receiver to tell if it was written by you, or someone who works for you.*
- *E-greetings are okay to send to friends but should not be sent to clients, colleagues, or business associates.*

WAYS TO SAY THANK YOU

It's not necessary to wait until someone does something nice for you before you express your thanks. Here are some other ways to be proactive and say thank you to those who contribute to your personal or professional success.

Personalize holiday cards. If you plan to send out preprinted holiday cards with a company greeting, personalize them by writing a brief note and signing your name. This gives the card more meaning and makes the recipient feel special. For example, you might write, "Really enjoyed working with you during our annual conference. I wish you and your company much success in the coming year." Or, "Thank you for all your hard work this year. You're a strong asset to our team."

Celebrate special occasions. Instead of sending traditional cards and gifts during the holidays, keep in touch during other times of the year. "Happy Fourth of July" or "Happy New Year" cards can make you stand out. Send a gift that helps someone commemorate their own special occasion. Martha Rogers, Ph.D., of the Peppers & Rogers Group says she enjoyed receiving a photo scrapbook as a business thank you. This was something her whole family could enjoy rather than yet another notebook cover or desk clock. Whenever a client or colleague gives birth or adopts a child, she likes to send a baby gift.

Send fun or unique gifts. The more unusual the gift, the more memorable you will be. One of my clients, who owns and operates a New York PR firm, sends notes of thanks with plush bird toys made by Wild Republic (found online at *www.wildrepublic.com* and in stores around the United States). "Each toy has an authentic bird call. People go crazy over them," she says. "It has really made a difference in my business."

When you take the time to find out what your client will enjoy and use, your gift will make a greater impact. Katherine Catlin of the Catlin & Cookman Group was ecstatic when she received a quirky purple coffeepot from one of her clients. When she and her client were having breakfast together one morning, she commented on how much she liked the pot the server was using. Six weeks later, a purple coffeepot arrived in the mail. "I was impressed that my client thought enough to surprise me with something he knew I really liked and would appreciate. It was very rewarding," says Catlin.

For those people who seem to have everything, Nancy Brinker recommends sending a note saying, "In honor of your special occasion, a donation has been made to your favorite charity." This impresses your client or associate and helps others in need at the same time. Lillian Vernon likes to send Fruit-of-the-Month-Club gifts. "The fruit is always the finest quality and I'm promoting healthy eating habits at the same time," says Vernon. The company, Harry and David (*www.harryanddavid.com*), offers a superior monthly package as well as gourmet gift baskets and gift cards.

Embrace feedback. Research indicates that the majority of dissatisfied clients, customers, and employees don't bother to complain, they simply do business elsewhere or find another employment opportunity. Don't view negative feedback as a bad thing. Complaints can be a valuable gift in providing insight into your level of customer care and employee satisfaction. Survey your customers, clients, and employees occasionally to ensure that you are treating them the way they want to be treated. Give them a discount or enter their name in a drawing for a nice gift if they fill out or mail their comment card back to you by a specific date. You'll learn a lot about what others think of your company, product, service, or management style if you give them a chance to express their opinions and make suggestions.

Thank those you won't be working with. With clients and customers, it's easy to remember to write a note when you get the business. But that is seldom done when you don't get it. A thank-you note can also attract a client who is undecided about choosing your company, product, or service over another.

Sprint Store Management Vice President James Mickey says if a potential customer chooses not to do business with you, or if an applicant isn't chosen for a job, send a note of appreciation anyway. In the case of a lost customer, Mickey recommends saying, for example, "Thank you for the opportunity to earn your business. Sorry that our recommended solution was not selected. In the event that the other company should fail to meet your expectations, we would love the opportunity to earn your business in the future. Or, if you know of anyone else who could use our service, we would appreciate the referral." Mickey has seen customers come back and do business with his company one or two years later because he took the time to send a personal note, making them feel important and appreciated. All job applicants should be acknowledged with a note thanking them for their time and interest in the company, regardless of whether or not they get the job.

Thank those who help you build your business. Your business will grow and prosper when customers recommend you to others and employees make your customers happy by doing an outstanding job. Whenever a client refers business to you or one of your employees has an excellent performance review, say thank you by giving the person a small gift or a handwritten note. Validation for a job well done is often reciprocated with hard work or a deeper sense of loyalty. Most everyone will appreciate a gift certificate to their favorite restaurant or day spa, or tickets to a Broadway show or a concert, sporting event, or festival. A friend of mine who is a freelance writer keeps a supply of Starbucks gift cards on hand; whenever she wants to express her thanks to an employee, colleague, or client, she sends a gift card along with a handwritten note that reads, "Thanks a latte." Employees will appreciate time off, a bonus check, or a plane ticket to visit family members for the holidays. You'll find that gifts are less expensive in the long run than the cost to replace an employee.

Attending social events occasionally with clients or employees can foster goodwill by providing a more relaxed atmosphere in which to get acquainted on a more personal level. For decades, executives have seen that golf outings offer an idyllic setting in which to develop relationships. The lulls and pace of the game provide many opportunities to build camaraderie, talk business, or close the deal.

Stay connected after a sale. The success of your business may be directly related to the amount of client or customer contact after a sale. Thank-you notes and e-mails are an effective way to let others know you're thinking about them. Steve Leveen, cofounder and CEO of Levenger, a catalog, Internet, and retail company in Delray Beach, Florida, says writing thank-you notes is a highlight of his day. Leveen sends an average of ten notes a week. This is his way of staying in touch with his four stores' top twenty-five customers. "I send hundred-dollar gift cards and call my VIP customers just to thank them for their business and let them know when I'll be in town," says Leveen. "If they stop by one of my stores, I like to thank them in person."

Throw a party. Say "Thanks for your business" or "a job well done" by throwing a party or hosting an annual luncheon for your customers, coworkers, vendors, or special clients. A casual event, such as a barbecue or a luau, can be a great way to reconnect and get to know each other better.

Give a status report. If someone you know or work with performs a good deed, refers a piece of business to you, or offers good advice, write a note to let the person know how it turned out, even if you don't get the job, the promotion, or the piece of business.

Don't wait for a rainy day. Don't wait to contact someone when you're in need of a reference or favor, when you're looking for a new job, or when you're having a problem. "It's astonishing how many people forget to say thank you for helping them find a job," says Jeffrey Fox of Fox & Company. "They don't understand why you won't help them again when they're looking for their next job." You give relationships a chance to grow when you keep in touch. And when you do need help, in some cases the person may even offer to e-mail or make a follow-up phone call for you if you don't hear anything from a new contact.

GRATITUDE AND GRATUITIES

One way to show your appreciation while traveling or dining is by giving a gratuity, commonly known as a tip. The word "tip" is an acronym for "to insure promptness" or "to insure prompt service." Every time you embark on a personal or business trip, you encounter numerous opportunities to tip those who help you along the way. However, if you aren't familiar with certain tipping practices, you may, from time to time, wonder about what's correct, appropriate, or even expected.

Michael Lynn, an associate professor of consumer behavior and marketing at Cornell University's School of Hotel Administration, was surprised when he conducted a research study and discovered that approximately 30 percent of Americans are unaware that it is customary to tip a restaurant server 15 to 20 percent of the bill. Lynn, who has written more than twenty-five publications on the topic of tipping, found that a fair number of that 30 percent said, "I leave a buck or two."

Issues of tipping, of course, go far beyond restaurants. Americans, though still regarded internationally as the most generous tippers, have always had an uneasy feeling about when and how much to tip. Giving a gratuity is an important, yet voluntary, way to show someone your appreciation. In some cases, the amount you give can make the difference between receiving good service and great service. Here are some tipping-etiquette guidelines:

tipping at the airport

- Skycaps: $1 to $2 per bag. Tip more if the bag is bigger or heavier than usual.
- Taxi drivers: 10 to 15 percent of the bill.
- Sedans and limousines: 20 percent of the bill.
- Van driver for a rental car company: $1 per bag. Tip more if the bag is bigger or heavier than usual.

tipping at a hotel

- Doorman: $1 to $2 per bag for taking your bags out of the car and putting them onto the bell cart; $1 to $2 for hailing a taxicab on the street.
- Bellman: $1 to $2 per bag, depending on size and weight of your bags; $1 to $2 for every package or delivery to your room.
- Concierge: $5 to $10 for special services or favors, such as securing hard-to-get theater tickets or reservations to a popular restaurant.

- Housekeeper: $2 to $3 per night. If you ask your housekeeper to perform any type of special service, such as bringing extra towels or toothpaste and toothbrush, tip an additional $1 to $2. On the last day of your stay, place the money in an envelope, label it "Housekeeping," and put it in a place where it can easily be seen, either on a pillow or on the bathroom counter.
- Room service attendant: 15 to 18 percent of the bill before taxes. If the service charge is included in the bill, an extra gratuity is optional.

tipping for valet services

- If you elect to use a hotel, restaurant, or shopping mall's valet service, tip $2 to $3 each time the attendant retrieves your car. Overnight parking charges will be additional.

tipping at a restaurant

- If you check your coat, hat, or umbrella, tip $1 to $2 per item.
- Maitre d': $10 to $100, depending on the occasion, the restaurant, and the level of service you wish to receive. Present the tip before you sit down at your table.
- Waitstaff: 15 to 20 percent of the bill before taxes; 20 percent or more for exceptional service and at least 20 percent for parties of six or more or when dining in an upscale restaurant.
- Wine sommelier: tipping is optional. However, if your party is large and you order multiple bottles of wine and the sommelier is extremely helpful and attentive, consider giving 5 to 10 percent of the wine charge.
- Restroom attendant: 50¢ to $1 for handing you a towel, or if you use any products or cosmetics displayed on the sink.

Overall, tipping is discretionary and the amount is entirely up to you. In most circumstances, tipping is the best way to show your appreciation for what someone has done for you and how you have benefited from their service. When you give from the heart you will feel good, and those you tip will always appreciate your generosity.

The power of positive thanking is so strong it can open doors of opportunity and strengthen relationships. The act of giving and showing appreciation is desperately lacking in business today. So those of us who create unique ways to express our thanks to clients, colleagues, and coworkers are more likely to see positive results.

TIPS FROM THE TOP

Sending a late thank-you note is better than not sending a note at all.

Send cards during nontraditional holidays.

Show your appreciation to those who send you referrals.

Don't wait until you're down and out or need a favor to get in touch with someone.

Generously tip those who take good care of you or who make your life easier.

SOME FINAL THOUGHTS

*T*he essence of etiquette is courtesy and consideration, and the greatest courtesy we can give others is the warmth of our friendliness. As long as we are considerate of others' feelings, opinions, and values, we are exercising the innate courtesy on which all good manners are based. The circumstances in the workplace will continue to evolve rapidly, but the way in which we interact with others in kindness and consideration should never change.

We all have the ability and common sense to be our best selves. Hal Urban once said that people are inherently good—we just don't get credit for it. In *Life's Greatest Lessons* he writes, "I happen to believe that the overwhelming majority of people in the world are law-abiding, loving, and caring. They just don't get any publicity for it. Being good does not make the news."

When we give our coworkers, clients, and customers the best we have, we set ourselves apart from the competition and create long-lasting professional relationships. I believe speaker and author Kent M. Keith exemplifies what business class is all about in "The Paradoxical Commandments."

The Paradoxical Commandments

1. People are illogical, unreasonable, and self-centered. Love them anyway.
2. If you do good, people will accuse you of selfish ulterior motives. Do good anyway.
3. If you are successful, you will win false friends and true enemies. Succeed anyway.
4. The good you do today will be forgotten tomorrow. Do good anyway.
5. Honesty and frankness make you vulnerable. Be honest and frank anyway.
6. The biggest men and women with the biggest ideas can be shot down by the smallest men and women with the smallest minds. Think big anyway.
7. People favor underdogs but follow only top dogs. Fight for a few underdogs anyway.
8. What you spend years building may be destroyed overnight. Build anyway.
9. People really need help but may attack you if you do help them. Help people anyway.
10. Give the world the best you have and you'll get kicked in the teeth. Give the world the best you have anyway.*

*"The Paradoxical Commandments" by Kent M. Keith copyright © 1968, renewed 2001 by Kent M. Keith and reprinted by permission.

suggested readings and recommended web sites

BOOKS

Andre, Mary Lou. *Ready to Wear: An Expert's Guide to Choosing and Using Your Wardrobe*. New York: Perigee Books, 2004.

Axtell, Roger E., ed. *Do's and Taboos around the World*. 3rd ed. New York: Wiley, 1993.

———. *Do's and Taboos around the World for Women in Business*. New York: Wiley, 1997.

———. *Do's and Taboos of Hosting International Visitors*. New York: Wiley, 1990.

———. *Gestures: The Do's and Taboos of Body Language around the World*. New York: Wiley, 1998.

Baldrige, Letitia. *Letitia Baldrige's New Complete Guide to Executive Manners*. New York: Rawson, 1993.

———. *Letitia Baldrige's New Manners for New Times: A Complete Guide to Etiquette*. New York: Scribner, 2003.

Beckwith, Harry. *Selling the Invisible: A Field Guide to Modern Marketing*. New York: Warner Books, 1997.

————. *What Clients Love: A Field Guide to Growing Your Business.* New York: Warner Books, 2003.

Brown, Robert E., and Dorothea Johnson. *The Power of Handshaking: For Peak Performance Worldwide.* Herndon, Virginia: Capitol Books, 2004.

Carducci, Bernardo J. *The Pocket Guide to Making Successful Small Talk: How to Talk to Anyone, Anytime, Anywhere, about Anything.* New Albany, Indiana: Pocket Guide Pub., 1999.

Catlin, Katherine, and Jana Matthews. *Leading at the Speed of Growth: Journey from Entrepreneur to CEO.* Cleveland, Ohio: Hungry Minds, 2001.

Charles, C. Leslie. *Why Is Everyone So Cranky?: The Ten Trends Complicating Our Lives and What We Can Do about Them.* New York: Hyperion, 1999.

Corcoran, Barbara. *Use What You've Got: And Other Business Lessons I Learned from My Mom.* New York: Portfolio, 2003.

Covey, Stephen R. *The 7 Habits of Highly Effective People: Powerful Lessons in Personal Change.* Rev. ed. New York: Free Press, 2004.

Dresser, Norine. *Multicultural Manners: New Rules of Etiquette for a Changing Society.* New York: Wiley, 1996.

Feinberg, Steven L., ed. *Crane's Blue Book of Stationery: The Styles and Etiquette of Letters, Notes, and Invitations.* New York: Doubleday, 1989.

Forni, P. M. *Choosing Civility: The Twenty-five Rules of Considerate Conduct.* New York: St. Martin's Press, 2002.

Fox, Jeffrey J. *How to Become a Rainmaker: The Rules for Getting and Keeping Customers and Clients.* New York: Hyperion, 2000.

Horn, Sam. *Tongue Fu!: How to Deflect, Disarm, and Defuse Any Verbal Conflict.* New York: St. Martin's Press, 1996.

————. *What's Holding You Back?: 30 Days to Having the Courage and Confidence to Do What Your Want, Meet Whom You Want, and Go Where You Want.* New York: St. Martin's Press, 1997.

Innis, Pauline B., Mary Jane McCaffree, and Richard M. Sands. *Protocol: The Complete Handbook Of Diplomatic, Official & Social Usage.* 25th anniversary ed. Dallas, Texas: Durban House, 2002.

Isaacs, Florence. *Business Notes: Writing Personal Notes that Build Professional Relationships.* New York: Clarkson Potter, 1998.

————. *Just a Note to Say—: The Perfect Words for Every Occasion.* New York: Clarkson Potter, 1995.

Johnson, Dorothea. *The Little Book of Etiquette.* Philadelphia: Running Press, 1997.

Johnson, Larry, and Bob Phillips. *Absolute Honesty: Building a Corporate Culture that Values Straight Talk and Rewards Integrity.* New York: AMACOM, 2003.

Kaplan Thaler, Linda, and Robin Koval, with Delia Marshall. *BANG: Getting Your Message Heard in a Noisy World.* New York: Currency/Doubleday, 2003.

Levine, Michael. *Guerrilla P.R.: How You Can Wage an Effective Publicity Campaign—Without Going Broke.* New York: Harper-Business, 1993.

Lieberman, Simma; George F. Simons, and Kate Berardo. *Putting Diversity to Work: How to Successfully Lead a Diverse Workforce.* Menlo Park, California: Crisp Learning, 2004.

Lucas, James, R. *Fatal Illusions: Shredding a Dozen Unrealities that Can Keep Your Organization from Success.* New York: AMACOM, 1997.

————. *The Passionate Organization: Igniting the Fire of Employee Commitment.* New York: AMACOM Books, 1999.

Mackay, Harvey. *Swim with the Sharks without Being Eaten Alive: Outsell, Outmanage, Outmotivate, & Outnegotiate Your Competition.* New York: Morrow, 1998.

Mitchell, Jack. *Hug Your Customers: The Proven Way to Personalize Sales and Achieve Astounding Results.* New York: Hyperion, 2003.

Morrison, Terry; Wayne A. Conaway, and George A. Borden. *Kiss, Bow, or Shake Hands: How to Do Business in Sixty Countries.* Holbrook, Massachusetts: B. Adams, 1994.

Peppers, Don, and Martha Rogers. *Return on Customer: Maximizing the Value of Your Scarcest Resource.* Currency/Doubleday, 2005.

Ries, Al, and Laura Ries. *The Origin of Brands: Discover the Natural Laws of Product Innovation and Business Survival.* New York: HarperCollins, 2004.

Trump, Donald J. *Think Like a Billionaire: Everything You Need to Know About Success, Real Estate, and Life.* New York: Random House, 2004.

————. *Trump: How to Get Rich.* New York: Random House, 2004.

Urban, Hal. *Life's Greatest Lessons: 20 Things that Matter.* New York: Simon & Schuster, 2003.

————. *Positive Words, Powerful Results: Simple Ways to Honor, Affirm, and Celebrate Life.* New York: Simon & Schuster, 2004.

Visser, Margaret. *The Rituals of Dinner: The Origins, Evolutions, Eccentricities, and Meaning of Table Manners.* New York: Grove Weidenfeld, 1991.

Vitale, Joe. *The Attractor Factor: 5 Easy Steps for Creating Wealth (or Anything Else) From the Inside Out.* New York: John Wiley & Sons, 2005.

Von Drachenfels, Suzanne. *The Art of the Table: A Complete Guide to Table Setting, Table Manners, and Tableware.* New York: Simon & Schuster, 2000.

Williams, Pat. *Coaching Your Kids to Be Leaders: The Keys to Unlocking Their Potential.* New York: Warner Faith, 2004.

Zraly, Kevin. *Windows on the World Complete Wine Course: 2005 Edition.* New York: Stirling, 2004.

WEB SITES

Brooks Brothers	*www.brooksbrothers.com*
Crane & Company	*www.crane.com*
CultureGrams	*www.culturegrams.com*

Culturosity	*www.culturosity.com*
Escada	*www.escada.com*
Executive Planet	*www.executiveplanet.com*
Harry and David	*www.harryanddavid.com*
Mitchells/Richards	*www.mitchellsonline.com*
National Speakers Association	*www.nsaspeaker.org*
Toastmasters	*www.toastmasters.org*
Uncorked! Magazine	*www.uncorkedmagazine.com*
Waterman Pens	*www.waterman.com*
Wild Republic	*www.wildrepublic.com*

acknowledgments

The late Christopher Reeve once said, "So many of our dreams at first seem impossible, then they seem improbable, and then, when we summon the will, they soon become inevitable." One person can write a book, but it takes many caring people to make it come to life. For me, giving birth to this book has been a dream come true. There were growing pains every step of the way, but each one was well worth the effort. Writing this book has given me more pride, knowledge, and confidence than any other project I've ever tackled.

Brian Gleason, my husband, thank you for your patience, encouragement, and love. Without your help, I never could have taken the time off to devote to this book. I especially appreciate your willingness to withstand my long hours and late nights in the office so I could complete it.

A world of thanks to Rita Rosenkranz. You've been so much more than just a literary agent. It was my good fortune that you and I met when we did at the Maui Writers Conference. You helped simplify the complexities of the literary world for me. I am deeply grateful for your integrity, guidance, accessibility, and belief in this book.

My gratitude goes out to the fine people at St. Martin's Press, and especially to my executive editor, Sheila Curry Oakes. Thanks to your judgment and foresight, the material in the book was broadened to benefit a wider audience. Thanks to my copy editor, Janet Fletcher, for your professionalism and extraordinary attention to detail, and to Julie Mente for keeping me on track and organized and for doing what needed to be done behind the scenes. A great big thank-you to my talented publicist, Joe Rinaldi, for your outstanding marketing skills. I'm honored to be on the same team with all of you.

C. Leslie Charles, you're simply the best book doctor. You were a gentle critic and editor, a trusted adviser, and an exemplary teacher. Thank you for providing me with motivation when I needed it most. To Sasheika Tomlinson, Cathy Beals, and Marilyn Murray Willison for providing the administrative support for this project, and to Harry Beckwith for seeing the importance of my message and generously giving your time and talents to provide an outstanding foreword for this book.

Dorothea Johnson, thank you for taking me under your wing and giving so much of yourself. I am proud to be one of your students. The education I received from you helped create the foundation for this book. Your wisdom and guidance inspired me to take my business to a higher level and put my passion on paper so that a new generation of executives could benefit from business etiquette. You'll always hold a special place in my heart.

To good friends Dale Carlson, who believed in my writing abilities long before I dreamed of owning my own business, and Dr. Susan Lee, thank you for your friendship, precious advice, and enthusiasm for the book.

Thanks to photographer Ted West, makeup artist Tami Crosby, and Gregory Boyajian, C.D.T., M.D.T., D.D.S., for helping me look my very best, and to Shannon McRae, manager of Escada in Palm Beach, for generously providing me with a gorgeous suit to wear for my book photograph.

Thank you to all the generous people quoted in these pages, and to those who are not in the book who devoted their time and wisdom to making this book more insightful. I gained an advanced degree simply by listening to all of your wonderful stories. Many thanks to Gary Aldrich, Stacy Allison, Mary Lou Andre, Roger Axtell, Bob Barrett, Kate Berardo, Nancy Brinker, Bernardo Carducci, Katherine Catlin, Neil Cavuto, C. Leslie Charles, Ryan Conrad, Victor Coppola, Barbara Corcoran, Bob Danzig, Paul Donahue, Jancee Dunn, Keith Ferrazzi, Coleman Finkel, Margie Fisher, the Honorable Mark Foley, P. M. Forni, Jeffrey Fox, Richard Glovsky, Sam Horn, Larry Johnson, David Jones, Linda Kaplan Thaler, Wendy Lang, Steve Leveen, Michael Levine, James Lucas, Michael Lynn, Harvey Mackay, William Mahoney, James Mickey, Jack Mitchell, Mitzi Perdue, Bob Pyke, Al Ries, Colette Robicheau, Martha Rogers, Mark Spivak, Eric Strauss, Patricia Thorp, Gayle Treutel, Jack Trout, Donald Trump, Hal Urban, Lillian Vernon, Joe Vitale, Steve Watts, Pat Williams, and Monsignor Robert Wolff.

Finally, I'm blessed to work with a terrific group of corporate clients, college students, and newsletter subscribers who know how vital business etiquette is in the workplace and in life in general. You continue to quench my thirst for knowledge by teaching me what I need to know, when I need to know it. For that I am grateful.

index

about the author

JACQUELINE WHITMORE is the founder of the Protocol School of Palm Beach, a company specializing in business etiquette, techno-etiquette, and international protocol. She is also the Cell Phone Etiquette Spokesperson for Sprint and the founder of National Cell Phone Courtesy Month, which is in July. Prior to starting her company, Jacqueline spent more than fourteen years in the hospitality and tourism industry. She served as the publicist and protocol officer for the Breakers Hotel in Palm Beach, where she handled media relations and advised hotel personnel on the nuances of dealing with royalty, celebrities, and other VIPs. Jacqueline and her husband, Brian Gleason, live in Florida.

For information about Jacqueline's seminars, contact her at:

The Protocol School of Palm Beach, Inc.
Post Office Box 3073
Palm Beach, Florida 33480
Phone: (561) 586-9026
E-mail: info@etiquetteexpert.com
Web site: www.etiquetteexpert.com